YESTERDAY'S REFLECTIONS

YESTERDAY'S REFLECTIONS

A Repository of Memories

Short Stories

Devotionals

Poems

Lessons

ALBERT F. SCHMID

iUniverse, Inc.
Bloomington

Yesterday's Reflections
A Repository of Memories

iUniverse books may be ordered through booksellers or by contacting:

iUniverse
1663 Liberty Drive
Bloomington, IN 47403
www.iuniverse.com
1-800-Authors (1-800-288-4677)

ISBN: 978-1-4759-7377-8 (sc)
ISBN: 978-1-4759-7379-2 (hc)
ISBN: 978-1-4759-7378-5 (ebk)

Printed in the United States of America

iUniverse rev. date: 02/21/2013

PREFACE

Dedications and Disclaimers

Writing a book is like looking into a mirror and transforming the image to the written word. Someone once said a picture is worth a thousand words. The biblical writer, David proclaims, **"Your word . . . a light for my path."** Psalm 119: 105 NIV. In order to see and understand the word we must have light and that light comes from the Lord.

Very little is needed to make a happy life. It merely depends on yourself, all that is within you, in your way of thinking and your relationship with God. I consider myself blessed because I have been given the opportunity to live a happy life.

It is wonderful to be able to look back upon my past with reflection to share some of the memories and stories of which I write. I appreciate the encouragement and support which has come from The First Baptist Churches in Wickford and East Greenwich, Rhode Island.

My wife Audrey continues to be my number one critic and guide and provides the support and encouragement which is so important.

> **Coming together is a beginning;**
> **Keeping together is progress;**
> **Working together is success.**
> *Henry Ford*

Scriptural quotations are from the NIV (New International Version) Study Bible, 10th Anniversary Edition, Zondervan Corporation, unless otherwise indicated.

BLESSINGS

A blessing cannot be kept. If it is stopped with the recipient, then the blessing disappears.

We are blessed significantly in many ways, but particularly by being a member of the First Baptist Church of East Greenwich. The church provides us the opportunity to minister and evangelize while serving on the Visitation Committee and as Pastor of Eldercare and Nursing Home Ministries.

We are the recipients of a blessing and we need to keep the blessing working by being the source of the blessing to other people.

Rev. Albert F. Schmid
December 1, 2012

HOLIDAY ALMANAC

2013

JANUARY

	1	2	3	4	5
6	7	8	9	10	11	12
13	14	15	16	17	18	19
20	21	22	23	24	25	26
27	28	29	30	31		

FEBRUARY

					1	2
3	4	5	6	7	8	9
10	11	12	13	14	15	16
17	18	19	20	21	22	23
24	25	26	27	28		

MARCH

					1	2
3	4	5	6	7	8	9
10	11	12	13	14	15	16
17	18	19	20	21	22	23
24	25	26	27	28	29	30
31						

APRIL

1	2	3	4	5	6
7	8	9	10	11	12	13
14	15	16	17	18	19	20
21	22	23	24	25	26	27
28	29	30				

MAY

		1	2	3	4
5	6	7	8	9	10	11
12	13	14	15	16	17	18
19	20	21	22	23	24	25
26	27	28	29	30	31	

JUNE

						1
2	3	4	5	6	7	8
9	10	11	12	13	14	15
16	17	18	19	20	21	22
23	24	25	26	27	28	29
30						

JULY

1	2	3	4	5	6
7	8	9	10	11	12	13
14	15	16	17	18	19	20
21	22	23	24	25	26	27
28	29	30	31			

AUGUST

				1	2	3
4	5	6	7	8	9	10
11	12	13	14	15	16	17
18	19	20	21	22	23	24
25	26	27	28	29	30	31

SEPTEMBER

1	2	3	4	5	6	7
8	9	10	11	12	13	14
15	16	17	18	19	20	21
22	23	24	25	26	27	28
29	30					

OCTOBER

	1	2	3	4	5
6	7	8	9	10	11	12
13	14	15	16	17	18	19
20	21	22	23	24	25	26
27	28	29	30	31		

NOVEMBER

					1	2
3	4	5	6	7	8	9
10	11	12	13	14	15	16
17	18	19	20	21	22	23
24	25	26	27	28	29	30

DECEMBER

1	2	3	4	5	6	7
8	9	10	11	12	13	14
15	16	17	18	19	20	21
22	23	24	25	26	27	28
29	30	31				

HOLIDAY CONTENTS

DEVOTIONAL CONTENTS

HOLIDAY ALMANAC

A holiday is little more than an epithet of persons, places or events. Reflecting on the holiday, it is interesting to know the history, purpose and nature of the celebration and why it has been declared a national holiday. Holidays occur at a time that most people anticipate. It is a time that families wait for and make plans to observe. Travel plans and vacations often include the holiday that provides the time away from work or studies. Whether a child or an adult, public holidays hold a special place in our hearts. They signify a break from the routine and mundane ways of life.

Take a look at the listing of public holidays; check the month and dates of each and read the accompanying devotional thoughts for relevance. For example, considering all of the holidays for the year, in the United States, only two holidays honor a private person. Columbus Day which honors Christopher Columbus, the explorer, who discovered America and the Caribbean Islands in 1492, and Martin Luther King, Jr. who led the civil rights crusade in the late '60s. Of course, we recognize former U.S. Presidents, George Washington and Abraham Lincoln and honor them by declaring President's Day in February, close to their actual birthdays.

Many holidays have a religious connotation. They include: Shrove Tuesday (start of Mari Gras.) Ash Wednesday (beginning of Lent); Passover; Palm Sunday; Good Friday; Easter; Ramadan; Yon Kippur; Rosh Hashanah; Hanukkah, and Christmas.

Other holidays that are celebrated include; St. Patrick's Day; Valentine's Day: Labor Day; Memorial Day; Independence Day (4th of July); Flag Day; Patriots Day, Election Day; Halloween; Thanksgiving; Black Friday and Pearl Harbor. Also, don't forget the seasonal days, Spring, Summer, Fall and Winter. Be sure to adjust your clocks when Day Light Savings rolls around. Rule of thumb: Spring forward, Fall back.

When reading the list you will probably wonder how so many holidays came about. Many of the holidays were sponsored and encouraged by the Labor Unions so that workers would have additional time off from their work with pay.

NEW YEAR'S DAY

January 1st

New Year's Day is observed on January 1st, the first day of the year on the modern Gregorian calendar, as well as the Julian calendar used in ancient Rome. With most countries using the Gregorian calendar as their primary calendar, New Year's Day is the closest thing to being the world's only truly global public holiday. The New Year is often celebrated with fireworks at the stroke of midnight as the New Year starts January 1st.

The Romans dedicated the day to Janus, the God of gates, doors, and beginnings. After Julius Caesar reformed the calendar in 46 BC and was subsequently murdered, the Roman Senate voted to make a god of him and honor him on the first January in 42 BC to celebrate his life and his rationalized new calendar. The month originally owes its name to Janus, who had two faces, one looking forward and the other looking back. This suggests in some ways that the New Year's celebrations are founded on pagan traditions.

January 1st becomes a time for a fresh start in a new year after looking back at yesterday's reflections. The act of remembering the events of the passing year may help to alight in hope that the smoke emitted from the flames will bring new life to the world. New Year's Day is traditionally a feast, but since the turn of the century it has become an occasion to celebrate the evening before on New Year's Eve. There are fireworks at midnight after watching the ball on the clock in Times Square drop. Joyous parties and festivities are held. It is a new year with new hope for the future.

HAVE A HAPPY AND JOYOUS NEW YEAR!

BLUE MONDAY

The Third Monday in January

The New Year's parties are over. The bells and the whistles are silent. A few New Year's resolutions have been made and that many have been broken. The weather is cold and nasty and the world is off to making the new year another historic time.

The third Monday of the month is known as the Bluest Day of the year. A psychologist from Cambridge University in England, declared that the third Monday in January is the worst time for depression and he refers to it as **Blue Monday.**

Depression is a state of being depressed, dispirited, or melancholy. It is also defined as, "The time when we do without the things our parents never had."

The third Monday in January was chosen because:

1. The Christmas Holidays and New Year's partying is over. Time to get back to normal.
2. The weather is often at its worst. Cold, with snow and ice. Plain nasty.
3. The bills that we charged on our credit cards have arrived. They need to be paid.
4. And we have very likely broken all of our New Year's resolutions.

As a culture, we do not celebrate January 1st from some Judean-Christian obligation or custom. Instead, we wave-off the pagan cloud that hangs over New Year's Eve and we pause to thank God for another year of life and another year of promises. We look forward with high expectation.

The practice of making New Year's resolutions goes back over 3000 years to the ancient Babylonians. There is something about the start of the New Year that gives us the feeling of a **fresh-start** and a **new-beginning.** In reality, there is nothing sacred about December 31st, midnight or January

3

1, the first day of the new year. Nothing mystical occurs at midnight. So, what is wrong with making a New Year's resolution at **any** time, even on the 21st? As a Christian, if we decide to make a resolution then we should go ahead and do it. The question is how should it be done?

More common resolutions may include:
Lose weight.
Exercise regularly.
Eat healthier.

These are noble goals and are all good to set. However, **I Timothy 4:8** gives us some other instructions. Timothy says to keep exercise in perspective.

> *"Bodily exercise is all right, but spiritual exercise is far more important and is a tonic for all that you do."*
> **I Timothy 4:8 NIV**

The Jewish prophet, Micah rallies us in the direction of renewed character. Micah asks:

> *"What does the Lord require of you? To act justly, to love mercy, and to walk humbly with God."*

The following inscription is chiseled in the gateway at the **United States Naval Academy, at** Annapolis, Maryland: **"The Measure of a Man Is the Depth Of His Convictions, The Breadth Of His Interests and The Height of His Ideals."** And so it is with any person, a family, or even our nation.

> Philippians 4:13 says: *"I can do everything through Him who gives me strength."*

> John 15:5 declares: *"I am the vine, you are the branches. If a man remains in me and I in him, he will bear much fruit"*

If God is centered in our resolutions we have a good chance for success, depending on our commitment. If it is God's will for something to be fulfilled it will happen. If that resolution is not God honoring or is not in agreement with God's word we will not receive God's help.

If we are going to **Look Up** in this year we need to focus on our walk with God, not keeping up with the Joneses.

If we are going to **Look Down** in let us not see our cup half empty, but consider those who live on less than $2 per day and have much less than we have.

If we are going to **Look Out** we need to remember the words of Mother Teresa who said, "We cannot do great things . . . only small things with great Love."

Then what sort of resolution should we make?

1. Pray to the Lord for wisdom in regards to what we should resolve.
2. Pray for wisdom as to how to fulfill the goals that God gives us.
3. Rely on God's strength to help us.
4. Find an accountability partner who will help us and encourage us.
5. Don't be proud or vain. Give God the glory.

"Commit your ways to the LORD, trust also in Him."

MARTIN LUTHER KING DAY

Martin Luther King, Jr. Day is a United States federal holiday. It is observed on the third Monday of January. It is a floating holiday observed on a Monday rather than his birthday in accordance with the Uniform Monday Holiday Act passed by Congress.

The idea of Martin Luther King, Jr. Day as a holiday was promoted by the labor unions in contract negotiations. After King was assassinated in 1968 Representatives and Senators from Michigan and Massachusetts introduced a bill in Congress to make King's birthday a National Holiday. The bill came to a vote in 1979 but fell short of the numbers required for passage. Two main arguments against the bill were: (1) a paid holiday for federal employees would be too expensive, and (2) a holiday to honor a private citizen would be contrary to a long standing tradition. Only two persons have National Holidays honoring them. Christopher Columbus, the explorer whose voyages led to the discovery of America and the Caribbean Islands in 1492 and General George Washington who eventually became the first President of our country. There is now a special holiday in February named President's day which recognizes both Washington and Lincoln who have birthdays in February.

In 1980 musician Stevie Wonder spearheaded a campaign to recognize King by releasing a single record, "Happy Birthday," which popularized the endeavor. More than six million signatures were collected for a petition to Congress to enact the law. The petition, an effort in favor of the issue, was thought to be the largest is U.S. history.

President Ronald Reagan reluctantly signed the bill in November 1983, knowing that there were enough votes in Congress that his veto would be overturned. A holiday to honor King was established and was first observed on January 20, 1986. Since that time there have been a series of incidents voicing reluctance to observe the holiday.

- Senator Helms from North Carolina lobbied against the bill. He claimed that King was against the Vietnam War and that he was espousing "Action-oriented Marxism."
- President Reagan opposed the bill because of federal labor costs.
- Senator John McCain opposed the holiday because Arizona's Governor Evan Mecham refused to honor it.
- In 1989 Arizona replaced Columbus Day with Martin Luther King Day.
- New Hampshire created a "Civil Rights Day" in 1991 then changed it to Martin Luther King Day in 1999. They were the last State to name the holiday after Dr. King.
- Overall, by 2007 33 percent of all employers gave their employees the day off as a holiday.
- There are still arguments about the holiday:
  - (a) the holiday occurs about two weeks after the Christmas, New Year holiday and
  - (b) many school schedules are disrupted because the children are just returning from long year-end vacation time.

The King Holiday and Service Act, co-authored by Pennsylvania Senator Harris and Georgia Congressman Lewis, challenged all Americans to transform the King Holiday into a day of citizen action with volunteer service in honor of Dr. King. Since 1996 the annual Greater Philadelphia King Day of Service has been the largest event in the nation honoring Dr. King.

Honor Dr. Martin Luther King, Jr.

SHROVE TUESDAY

Tuesday February

Shrove Tuesday is known by several other names; **Pancake Day, Pancake Tuesday, Mardi Gras,** and **Fat Tuesday.** It is the day preceding Ash Wednesday, the first day of Lent. Shrove Tuesday is observed mainly in English speaking counties but is also observed in the Philippines and Germany. Shrove Tuesday is linked to **Easter**, so the date changes each year. Shrove Tuesday is always the day before Ash Wednesday which begins a period of fasting and a time of repentance.

The word shrove is past tense of the English verb shrive, which means to obtain absolution for one's sins through confession and doing penance. Shrove Tuesday gets its name from the shriving that English Christians were expected to do in preparation for Lent. They expected to receive absolution before Lent began. Shrove Tuesday is the last day of "shrovetide" and is somewhat analogous to a *Carnival* tradition that developed in countries of Latin America and Europe. For example Marti Gras. The term **"Shrove Tuesday"** is seldom used in the USA outside of liturgical traditions. It may be better known as Pancake Day, Margi Gras, or Fat Tuesday.

In most societies, the day is better known for the custom of eating pancakes before the start of Lent. Pancakes are chosen to be eaten because they are made from ingredients consisting of sugar, fat, milk, flour and eggs. Consumption of these rich foodstuffs was inconsistent with the traditionally restricted diets during the ritual fasting associated with Lent. The liturgical fasting dictated eating plainer foods and refraining from eating foods that would give pleasure. In many cultures this means no meat, no dairy products and no eggs. The fasting season lasted 40 days, from Ash Wednesday till Easter.

Many churches take advantage of Pancake Day and host fund-raising suppers consisting of pancakes, ham and sausages. Usually these dinners are well attended and are very successful but the purpose of making money exceeds the intent of Christians preparing to fast during Lent.

ASH WEDNESDAY

Wednesday February

Ash Wednesday is the day that **Lent** begins. **Ash Wednesday** is not a *holy day of obligation,* but many people would not think of letting Ash Wednesday go by without a trip to church to be marked with an ashen cross on their foreheads. Even people who seldom go to church at other times of the year may make a concerted effort to come for the ashes.

The official name of Ash Wednesday is the **"The Day of Ashes"**. The reason the day became known as Ash Wednesday is that it is forty days before **Good Friday,** and will always be on a Wednesday. The Bible does not mention either Lent or Ash Wednesday, but. the Bible does tell of the acts of repentance and supplication that were made by God fearing people.

The period of Lent is intended to be a time when sinful activities and habits are forsaken. **Ash Wednesday** is the "commencement" of this period of repentance. Perhaps you can remember some acts of repentance that you did. You may have given up eating ice cream or having a smoke, or drinking a beer, giving up going to the popular Friday Night movie, or eating that favorite dessert. And you were very compliant. Forty days is a long time.

The Bible contains numerous accounts of people using "dust and ashes" as a symbol of repentance and/or mourning. One example is Daniel, God's prophet who said:

> *"Then I turned to the Lord God and prayed and asked Him for help. I did not eat any food. To show my sadness I put on rough cloth and sat in ashes. I prayed to the Lord my God and told him about all of my sins." Daniel 9:3*

At the beginning of the 11th century it became a custom for all of the faithful to take part in a ceremony on the Wednesday before Lent that included the imposition of ashes. The tradition is that the sign of the cross is made in ashes on a person's forehead as a symbol of that person's identification with Jesus Christ.

Ash Wednesday, along with Lent is observed by most Roman Catholics, most Orthodox denominations and a number of Protestant denominations. Since the Bible does not command or condemn the procedure, a Christian is at liberty to prayerfully decide whether to observe **Ash Wednesday** or not. If you feel led to the Lord to observe Ash Wednesday and/or Lent the important thing is to have a Biblical perspective. It is good to repent of sinful activities. It is good to clearly identify yourself as a Christian. But we should not believe that God will automatically bless us in response to the observing of a ritual.

God is interested in our hearts, not in our doing rituals.

Remember that God loves us because of **who God is**, not because of **anything we did or did not do.**

Three things in Life that, once they are gone never come back:

1. Time
2. Words
3. Opportunity.

Three things in life that are never certain are:

1. Fortune
2. Success
3. Dreams

Three things that make a person significant are:

1. Commitment
2. Sincerity
3. Hard work

Three things that are truly "Constant"

FATHER,—SON—HOLY SPIRIT.

"I ask the Lord to bless you, as I prayed for you today,
To guide you and protect you, as you go along your way.
God's love is always with you, God's promises are true,
And when you give God all your cares,
You know that God will see you through."

Wednesday

At the beginning of the 11th century it became a custom for all of the faithful to take part in a ceremony on the Wednesday, 40 days before Easter, called Ash Wednesday. Easter is celebrated on the first Sunday after the full moon following the vernal equinox. That date varies between the 22nd of March and the 25th of April. Easter this year is Sunday, March 31. Lent begins on Wednesday February 13th.

Traditionally, on Ash Wednesday, the sign of the cross is made in ashes on a person's forehead as a symbol of that person's relationship with Jesus Christ. The period of **Lent** is intended to be a time when sinful activities and habits are forsaken. Perhaps you can remember some vows that you took that may have been considered acts of repentance. You may have given up eating ice cream, or having a smoke, or drinking a beer, or going to a popular Friday night movie with your friends. And you were very compliant. Forty days seemed like a long time.

Lent is a journey of reconciliation. God is not interested in our doing rituals, He is interested in our hearts. Wouldn't it be interesting if we were marked so that others could identify with our well being? Since the Bible doesn't command us, or condemn us, for celebrating Lent, the Christian certainly is at liberty to prayerfully decide to observe Ash Wednesday or not. If you feel closer to the Lord by participating in, observing and celebrating the customs of Ash Wednesday and Lent, the important thing is to have a Biblical perspective. It is good to repent of sinful ways. It is also good to identify as a Christian. But we should never expect God to automatically bless us in response to our observing a ritual God is interested in our hearts, not in our doing rituals. Remember, God loves us because **of who God is . . . not because of anything we have or have not done.** *"Whoever believes* *and is baptized, will be saved, but whoever does not believe will be condemned."*

"God gives. We receive . . . and we are blessed. The Lord is good to all, he has compassion on all that he has made."

ST. VALENTINE'S DAY

February 14th

When we think of Valentine's Day we are conditioned to think of Cupid, Candy, Lacy hearts. and bouquets of flowers. Fancy cards and a holiday devoted to romantic love. Isn't it interesting that one of the best known Christian saints was a martyr for the Christian faith? St. Valentine's Day is not **Eros** or romantic, sexual love, but rather **Agape,** the selfless love for others and God.

There were three different Saint Valentines, all of them martyrs, mentioned in the early martyrologies for the date February 14th. One was a priest in Rome, another a bishop (of modern Terni) and the third was a martyr in Africa. Little is known about these early Christian men, except that, each died for the love of Christ.

The Golden Legend, a medieval book of stories about saints tells of a priest, **Valentine,** who was imprisoned by the Emperor Claudius II for leading people to Christ. While **Valentine** was being interrogated by a Roman officer, the priest preached **Christ** as the "One and Only Light". The officer who had a blind daughter, challenged Valentine to pray to Christ for his daughter's cure. The girl was cured, and the entire family was converted to Christianity. According to legend, while awaiting execution, Valentine wrote notes of instruction, affection and encourage-ment to the Christian community in Rome, and they were secretly delivered by a young boy who visited him in prison.

When we realize that the heart of Saint Valentine was, like other Christian martyrs, "pierced" by the love of Our Lord Jesus Christ, and that he shed his blood for this, it seems appropriate that the **red heart** is a symbol of this powerful love. We think about the power of the love of God—our love for Him—and His for us—and it inspires us to love one another. It is this kind of love that encourages the faithful Christian to accomplish deeds of extra-ordinary courage, even unto death, to bring the truth of faith to others.

14

On St. Valentine's Day, Christians have an opportunity for some real **enculturation,** that is planting seeds of Christ's truth into the cultures in which we live.

The popular customs of St. Valentine's Day probably originated in medieval Europe. It was common belief in England and France that on February 14th, which is half way through the second month of the year, the birds began to pair. This fostered a belief that "love birds" represented the day dedicated to lovers, and provided the proper occasion for writing love letters and sending lover's tokens.

There are many examples that can be used to illustrate Valentine's Day. But, never forget what the Bible says and the teachings of our Savior Jesus Christ.

There are many passages of the Bible that reflect God's love. One of the best known is: **John 3:16**

> *"For God so loved the world that he gave his only begotten Son, that whosoever believeth on Him should not perish, but have everlasting life."*

PRESIDENTS' DAY

February

Washington's Birthday is a United States federal holiday celebration. It is held on the third Monday of February in honor of General George Washington, the first President of the United States. The holiday is also commonly referred to as **Presidents' Day.**

As the first federal holiday to honor an American citizen the holiday was first celebrated on Washington's actual birthday, February 22nd. On January 1, 1971 the federal holiday was shifted to the third Monday in February by the Uniform Monday Holiday Act. This places it between February 15 and 21st, which make "Washington's Birthday" a misnomer since it never occurs on the actual date.

Since 1951 there has been attempts to name the holiday President's Day. Because of the proximity to Lincoln's birthday, February 12, it was decided that Washington's birthday, and a President's Day would be unduly burdensome and the idea was dropped. By the mid 1980s, advertisers suggested that the name President's Day could be used to observe both Washington and Lincoln's birthdays and more than a dozen states renamed the holiday, although it was never declared a federal holiday.

Today the Federal holiday, Presidents' Day, has become a well known day in which many stores, especially car dealerships hold giant sales. Until the late 1980s corporate businesses generally closed on the day, but more and more businesses began to remain open and the retailers continued to promote their business. Many public transit systems have gone to regular schedules. Even schools have classes on President's Day. Some schools elected to close for a single day, while others choose to take a "mid-winter recess" and close for the entire week beginning with the Monday holiday.

The holiday has a variety of things that are used to celebrate President's Day.

1. Alexandria, VA, Washington's hometown hosts a month long tribute.
2. Eustis, FL, has a "George Fest" held since 1902.
3. Westmoreland County VA. Washington's birthplace has public celebrations through the holiday weekend till February 22nd.
4. Alabama celebrates George Washington's birthday on the third Monday along with the birthday of Thomas Jefferson, who was born in April.
5. In Arkansas the third Monday is George Washington's birthday and Daisy Gatson Bates Day, an official State holiday.
6. In 2007 the USA celebrated Washington's 275th birthday and the 75th anniversary of the Purple Heart Medal.

LEAP YEAR

February 29, (Each four years)

In the **Gregorian Calendar,** the standard calendar used in most of the world today, most years that are divisible by 4 are known as **Leap years.** In a **leap year,** the month of February has **29 days** instead of 28. Adding an extra day to the calendar every four years compensates for the fact that a solar year is almost six hours longer than 365 days.

Why is it important to Christians that we have a **Leap year?** The Gregorian calendar was designed to keep the vernal equinox on or as close to March 21 as possible so that the date of **Easter** can be celebrated on the Sunday after the 14th day of the full moon that falls on or after the 21st of March. **Seasons and astronomical events** do not repeat at the exact number of full days, so a calendar which had the same number of days in each year would over time drift with respect to the events it was suppose to track. By occasionally inserting an additional day into the year the drift can be corrected. A year which is not a leap year is called a common year.

The 29th of February, in our leap year, is the day that make that adjustment. Anyone who celebrates their birthday on the 29th of February is unique. If that person, born on the 29th of February has celebrated seven birthdays in their life time they are 28 years of age. Ten birthdays would make them 40 years old, and twenty birthdays would mean that they would be 80 years old. Just think of all the ice cream and cake they have missed over that time.

My wife has a favorite expression; when someone asks her how old she is. Her answer is, **"I don't know how old I am, . . . except that I have had 80 birthdays."** That wouldn't work if she were a **Leaping person,** a person who was born on the 29th of February. She would have to say that she has had only 20 birthdays. Now that might not be so bad after all but might make it hard for others to believe.

"Blessed are the flexible, for they shall not be bent out of shape."

"Why are you downcast, O my soul?
Why so disturbed within me?
Put your hope in God, for I will
Yet praise him."

Psalm 42:11

DAYLIGHT SAVINGS TIME SPRING

Sunday in March

Daylight Savings is the practice of advancing clocks in the spring so that evenings have more daylight and mornings have less. Typically clocks are adjusted forward one hour near the start of spring and are adjusted backward in autumn. Though mentioned by Benjamin Franklin in 1784 the idea of daylight savings was first proposed in 1895 by George Vernon Hudson. It was implemented during the First World War. The practice has been both praised and criticized. Adding daylight to evenings benefits retailing, sports events, and other activities that exploit sunlight after working hours. But, it causes problems for evening entertainment and occupations tied to the sun. The original intent was to reduce evening usage of incandescent lighting and save on electricity.

DST clock shifts present other challenges. It complicates timekeeping, can disrupt meetings, confuses travelers, frustrates time zone transactions, and even affects sleep patterns. Most modern societies operate on the basis of "Standard Time". and are not governed by the movement of the earth in relation to the Sun. When standard time is applied year round a significant portion of the longer sunlight hours will fall in the early mornings while there may be longer periods of darkness in the evening. Not too bad for people who are early risers but for those who tend to sleep late the hours of sunlight are wasted. Obviously this works well in an agricultural society but is tough on kids going to school and parents who work in a factory.

Clock shifts are always scheduled on the weekend to avoid major disruption. If you are planning a trip to a neighboring time zone and the city to which you are traveling is on or near the line, double check to see if the community chooses to change to Daylight savings time. Now, if you are thoroughly confused just remember this rule-of-thumb:

Spring Forward . . . Fall Back.

ST. PATRICK'S DAY

Nestled among the religious traditions of Lent, is a holiday known as **St. Patrick's Day. Saint Patrick** was a Catholic priest who became revered by Christians for establishing the Catholic Church in Ireland in the **fifth century AD.**

Saint Patrick was born in Scotland in 387 and died in Ireland in 461 AD, at the age of 74. He is remember for his service to the church and to the citizens of the land. His anniversary is celebrated each year on March 17. Although the details of his life are unclear, most agree that he played a significant role in establishing Christianity in Ireland.

Lent is a period of fasting and a time for repentance traditionally observed by Catholics and some Protestant denominations, in preparation for Easter. The Lenten period was instituted in the **4th century** and has become a time of religious worship occurring 40 days before Easter. During this time people eat sparingly and give-up particular foods or habits. Ash Wednesday and Lent began as a way to remind people to repent of their sins in a manner similar to the way people in the Old Testament times repented. The use of the sackcloth, ashes, and fasting was the tradition.

Saint Patrick, born in Scotland, of religious Roman Catholic parents, was captured as a young boy of 16 years and sold into slavery in Ireland. He tended sheep for his very cruel master in the valley of Braid and on the slopes of Slemish. While tending the flocks, he prayed many times a day: the prayer called, **"The Love of God."** As his prayer life grew he told of what happened: His fear (the Lord's faith) increased in him more and more, the faith grew, the spirit was roused, so that in a single day he would say as many as a 100 or more prayers, and at night nearly the same number. He claimed that he felt no hurt from it, even with snow and ice or rain there was no slothfulness, because the spirit was fervent within him.

The beautiful prayer of St. Patrick is popularly known as **"St. Patrick's Breast-Plate."** and is translated from the old Irish text.

St. Patrick's Breast-Plate

I bind to myself today
God's Power to guide me.
God's Might to uphold me,
God's Wisdom to teach me,
God's Eye to watch over me,
God's Ear to hear me,

God's Word to give me speech,
God's Hand to guide me,
God's Way to lie before me,
God's Shield to shelter me,
God's Host to secure me
Against the snare of demons,

Against the seductions of vice,
Against the lusts of nature,
Against everyone who meditates injury to me,
Whether far or near,
Whether few or many.
Amen

About 432, St. Patrick returned to Ireland as a missionary and succeeded in converting many of the pagan tribes in the country to Christianity. Later in his life he wrote a brief text telling of his life and ministry. It is known as, *"The Confession of St. Patrick."*

St. Patrick's Day is a feast day in March and is celebrated as a day of **Irish Pride.** A popular folk tale says that St. Patrick chased all of the snakes from Ireland. But, there is no historical basis for this story. Another folk tale is that he used shamrocks to teach about the holy Trinity. Another myth. In Gaelic the saint's name is *Padraig.* Whether Catholic or not, I believe that we can all benefit by knowing of St. Patrick and living the examples that he set. Saying his prayer provides us with a blessing from God.

THE SEASONS SPRING STARTS

March 20

A **season** is a subdivision of the year, marked by changes in the weather, ecology and the hours of daylight. Seasons results from the annual revolution of the Earth around the Sun and the tilt of Earth's axis relative to the plane of revolution. Depending on the regions, the temperate region or the polar regions each are marked by changes in the intensity of sunlight.

During March, April and May in the northern hemisphere, temperatures begin to warm up because of the intensity of sunlight that reaches the Earth's surface. Animals who hibernate begin to stir, birds begin to migrate north, plants start to grow and the grass turns green. Punxsutory Phil, the ground hog from Pennsylvania comes out of his den, takes a look around and tells us if we are going to have another 6 weeks of winter.

So we call it Spring. Don't put away the snow shovel yet, but you might like to check your Farmer's Almanac for the best time to plant early peas and lettuce.

"I planted the seed, Apollo watered it, but God made it grow".
I Corinthians 3: 6 NIV

PALM SUNDAY

What happened on the first Palm Sunday? And why was it so important?

In late 1970's I was invited by Israeli Aircraft Industries to go to Israel and visit their aircraft production facilities at Tel Aviv Airport in Israel. The trip included a week of touring Israel, seeing the religious shrines and historic places of the Holy Lands, including Jerusalem. It was exciting and very educational.

As I stood at the Mount of Olives overlooking old Jerusalem, the walled city, I was reminded of how Jesus made His triumphal entry into the city. We discovered that all of the Muslim businesses were closed on Friday. Then on Saturday, the Sabbath, all of the Jewish shops were closed. On Sunday it was a celebration for many of the Christians, who gathered in the garden tomb at Calvary, to celebrate the resurrection of Jesus from the dead.

Recalling the events of Holy Week which began on Sunday, a week before Easter, I was reminded of the how we had traveled the same road that Jesus had taken from Jericho to Bethany and Bethpage, where he visited the home of Mary, Martha and Lazarus. How he had instructed two of his disciples to find a young donkey which had never been ridden so that he would fulfill prophecy by riding it into the city of Jerusalem on that memorial day.

Mark records in his gospel, chapter 11:1-11 these events of Palm Sunday:

> "As they approached Jerusalem and came to Bethpage and Bethany to the Mount of Olives, Jesus sent for two of his disciples saying to them; 'Go to the village ahead of you and as you enter it you will find a colt tied there, which no one has ever ridden. Untie it and bring it here. If anyone asks you, why are you doing this? Tell him the Lord needs it and will send it back here shortly. They went and found the colt outside in the

street, tied at a doorway. As they brought the colt to Jesus they threw their cloaks over it and he sat on it.

Many people spread their cloaks on the road while others spread branches that were cut from the field. Those who went ahead and those who followed shouted **Hosanna. Blessed is he who comes in the name of the Lord. Blessed is the coming kingdom of our father, David. Hosanna in the highest." Mark 11: 1-11. NI**

Jesus entered Jerusalem and went to the temple. He looked around at everything but it was already late, he went out to Bethany with the twelve to spend the night. This is the beginning of Holy Week.

"Jesus Christ is Lord to the Glory of God the Father."
Eph. 2:7. NIV

PASSOVER

Passover is a Jewish festival. It commemorates the story of the Exodus in which the ancient Israelites were freed from slavery from the Egyptians. Passover begins on the 15th day of the month of Nisan, depicted by the Jewish calendar. It is spring in the Northern Hemisphere and it lasts for seven to eight days. Passover is one of the most widely observed Jewish holidays of record.

In the Bible, old testament, the story of the Exodus tells of how God helped the Children of Israel escape the bondage suffered in Egypt by inflicting ten plagues upon the Egyptians Before the Pharaoh decided to release his Israelite slaves the people suffered terribly. The tenth and worst plague was the death of the Egyptian first-born. The Israelites were instructed to mark the doorposts of their homes with the blood of a spring lamb. The spirit of the Lord, seeing the blood knew to *pass over* these homes sparing the lives of the first-born child, hence the name of the holiday, **Passover**. Exodus 12:11-13.

When the Pharaoh pursued the Israelites they left their homes in such haste that they didn't take time to wait for bread dough to rise (leaven). In commemoration, no leavened bread is eaten during the Passover time. Therefore, the name, "The Festival of Unleavened Bread." Matzo (flat unleavened bread) is a symbol of the holiday and is used during the celebration.

In Jewish custom one or two festive Seder meals are celebrated. One is celebrated in the Temple in Jerusalem, the other for the Passover sacrifice. In Samaritan practice, men gather for a religious ceremony on Mount Gerizim and that ceremony includes the ancient cow Sacrifice.

The Christian feast of Maundy Thursday finds its roots in the Jewish Feast of the Passover. It was there in Jerusalem, in the upper room, that Jesus established the Lord's Supper.

As the apostles shared the Passover meal, Jesus prayed for their attention. He began to speak and Jesus said:

"A new commandment I give you . . . Love one another.
As I have loved you, so you must love one another.
By this all men will know you are my disciples, if you
Have love for one another.
By this all men will know that you are my disciples, if
You have love for one another."

John 13: 34 NIV

After they had eaten they sang some hymns and went out to the Garden of Gethsemane to pray. It was here that the soldiers came and after being identified by Judas, Jesus was arrested and taken into custody.

GOOD FRIDAY

It is Good Friday. The phrase "**Good Friday**" does not appear in the Bible and neither does the word "**Friday.**" The only day of the week given a name in the scriptures is the seventh day, **The Sabbath.** Other days of the week are designated as the first, second third and so on.

The term **Good Friday** is called by various names in different countries; Holy Friday, Black Friday, Great Friday, Long Friday and Silent Friday. According to Catholic dogma, which has been carried over into Protestant Churches, Jesus was killed on Friday and resurrected on Sunday morning.

Good Friday is a day of fasting created by the Roman Catholic Church in the 4th century A.D. (long after Jesus had died). The day is dedicated to commemorating the crucifixion and death of Jesus. Fasting consisted of eating only one meal a day but could be supplemented by small collations.

We experience the observances of Holy Week as we move from the joyous celebrations of Palm Sunday to the resurrection of our Lord. We are called to focus on the triumphal entry of Jesus through the Golden Gate into the city, followed by the suffering the humiliation, and death that is part of Holy Week.

It is important for us to place the propriety of the Resurrection and the promise of newness and everlasting life, against the background of death and endings. It is only in walking through the shadows and the darkness of Holy Week, recalling the sacrifices of Jesus on that fateful day we call Good Friday, that we can realize the horror and magnitude of sin and its consequences and how they were satisfied by the dying of Jesus on the cross. Thus we truly understand the light and the hope of Sunday morning, Resurrection Day.

There were a variety of events that clustered on the last day before Jesus was arrested. **Maundy Thursday.** The term "Maundy" comes from the Latin word *mandatum (from which we get our English word mandate.)* It was here on this day that Jesus washed the disciples feet to illustrate humility and servanthood. Then the last meal, which the disciples thought was the Passover meal, was eaten. It was here that Jesus established the **Lord's Supper.**

But he was betrayed by Judas, for thirty pieces of silver. The disciples were puzzled and were asking if it was one of them. Even as Jesus and his disciples came together to share the meal they already stood in the shadow of the cross. Jesus made a new covenant, as written in the book of John (John 13:34)

Jesus said:

> **"A new commandment I give to you . . . Love one another. As I have loved you, so you must love one another. By this all men will know that you are my disciples, if you have love for one another,"**
> **John 13:34 niv**

The scriptures tell us that after they had eaten they sang some hymns and then went out to the Garden of Gethsemane to pray. It was there that the soldiers came and arrested Jesus. He was taken to the house of the High Priest, Caiaphas, and persecuted. The High Priest didn't want Jesus' blood on his hands so he turned him over to Pontius Pilate, the governor who asked the people what they desired, and they shouted, **"Crucify Him. Crucify Him, Crucify Him."**

Beaten and scourged, mocked and insulted, tortured and made to carry his cross to Calvary Hill, Jesus was treated as a lowly criminal. He was nailed to the cross and placed between two other victims of the government. Good Friday services are often a series of Scripture readings which include the following as recorded in the Gospel traditions: These were the last words of Jesus on the cross:

Seven Last Words of Jesus.

> **"Father, forgiven them for they know not what they are doing."**
> **Luke 23:34**

> **"I tell you the truth this day you will be with me in paradise."**
> **Luke 23:43**

"Dear woman, here is your son."

John 19:26-27

"My God, my God why have you forsaken me?"

Matthew 27: 46

"I thirst."

John 19:28

"It is finished!"

John 19:30

"Father into your hands I commit my spirit."

Luke 23:46

At 3 PM Jesus died. Good Friday is not a day of celebration but of mourning, both for the death of Jesus and the sins of the world that his death represents. Yet, although Friday is a solemn time it is not without its own joy. For while it is important to place the resurrection against the darkness of Good Friday, likewise the somberness of Good Friday should always be seen with the hope and joy of Resurrection Sunday.

Halleluiah, He Lives, Our Savior Lives.

EASTER SUNDAY

Many Christians wonder about the traditions and customs of worship events leading up to Easter. We all have learned about how Jesus was crucified in Jerusalem after He was condemned by Pontius Pilate. How the people seemed to turn against him and how he died on a wooden cross at Calvary, a hill called Golgotha. Golgotha means "The place of the skull."

The crucifixion of Jesus fullfilled prophecy. God and Jesus knew exactly what had to be done and it was done. However, a number of things happened leading up to this time. Through the ages the church has established a number of "holy days," and events that lead to that fateful day in Jerusalem.

In the 11th century there was custom started by the church for all of the faithful to take part in a ceremony that we know as Ash Wednesday. This a time 40 days before Easter and is known as the beginning of Lent. During this time Christians observed the period by fasting, avoiding festivities, and performing acts of penance. Meat, fish, eggs, and milk products were strictly forbidden and only one meal a day was eaten. The making of a sign of the cross on a person's forehead was a symbol that the person identified with Jesus Christ.

Ash Wednesday was February 13th this year. It is not a high holy day or a day of obligation, but many Christian Church goers would not think of letting Ash Wednesday go by without a trip to church to be marked with t he ashes. Since the Bible doesn't command or condemn the procedure a believer is at liberty to prayerfully decide to observe this day if they wish. The important thing is to have a Biblical perspective. It is always good to repent of sinful ways, and it is good to identify yourself as a Christian. However, we should never believe that God will automatically bless us in response to observing a ritual. *God is interested in our hearts, not in our rituals. Remember, God loves us because of who God is . . . not because of anything we have or have not done.*

- Three things in life that once they are gone never come back . . .

Time, Words, and Opportunity.
- Three things in life are never certain . . .
Fortune, Success, and Dreams
- Three things that make a person significant . . .
Commitments, Sincerity, and Hard Work.

The Sunday before Easter is Palm Sunday. It marks the beginning of **Holy Week.** We know Palm Sunday was the day that Jesus made a triumphal entry into Jerusalem through the Golden Gate. The account was beautifully described by Matthew in Chapter 20: 17-19.

> *"While Jesus was going up to Jerusalem, he took the twelve disciples aside by themselves, and said to them on the way, 'See we are going up to Jerusalem and the Son of Man will be handed over to the chief priests and scribes and they will condemn him to death; they will hand him over to the Gentiles to be mocked and flogged and crucified; and on the third day he will be raised."* Matthew 20: 17-19.

And, as prophesied, he entered the city riding on a young colt. The people greeted Him with palm branches for they expected a new king, a messiah who would free them from the Roman bondage. While Jesus was in the city he went to the temple and drove out the money lenders and merchants. He cursed the fig tree. He was anointed and he learned more of the sinister plot to send him to the cross. On Thursday he instructed his disciples to prepare the Passover Meal. They met them in a place known as the Upper Room. It was here that Jesus instituted the **Lord's Supper.**

> *"While they were eating Jesus took a loaf of bread, and after blessing it he broke it, gave it to his disciples and said, 'Take, eat, this is my body.' Then he took the cup and after giving thanks he gave it to them, saying, 'Drink from it all of you; for this is my blood of the covenant, which is poured out for many for the forgiveness of sins. I tell you I will never again drink of this fruit of the vine until that day when I drink it new with you in my Father's kingdom"* Matthew 20: 17-19

When they had sung a hymn they went out to the Mount of Olives. Then the **betrayal.** Judas, one of Jesus' disciples, had sold out for 30 pieces of silver. The soldiers came and with a kiss from Judas the Son of Man was arrested and taken into custody. Jesus was taken before the high court and Caiaphas, the high priest began the inquiry. The charge was blasphemy, giving false witness. The court decided to find him guilty and condemned him to death.

The next morning Jesus was taken to the Governor, Pontius Pilate. Pilate was a politician. He wanted peace in the territory at any price. After a number of questions, that Jesus refused to answer, Pilate washed his hands of the matter and turned Jesus over to the people to crucify him.

Jesus was beaten and flogged and made to carry his cross up the hill to Calvary. And along side two other criminals he was hung on the cross. From noon until three in the afternoon darkness came over the land. And Jesus was heard to say "Eli, Eli le-ma sa-bach-tha-ni. "My God, My God, why have you forsaken me? Then the curtains of the temple were torn in two, the earth shook and rocks were split as Jesus took his final breath.

Because the Sabbath law required the body be taken down from the cross and be buried before sunset a rich man by the name of Arimathea volunteered his tomb for internment.

The government appointed guards to standby the tomb to secure its entrance. On Sunday, the first day of the week, Mary Magdalene and the other Mary went to the tomb but before they arrived an earthquake occurred and the stone was rolled away. When they looked into the tomb expecting to see Jesus' body they found the tomb was empty. Jesus had risen as he said he would.

Praise the Lord. Have a Happy Easter. He lives, we know He lives!

ARBOR DAY

The last Friday in April

The first Arbor Day was held on April 10, 1872 in Nebraska City, Nebraska. It was the brainchild of Julius Morton a Nebraskan journalist and politician. Morton served as Secretary of Agriculture under President Grover Cleveland. But his most important legacy was his idea of establishing a special day to be set aside dedicated to tree planting and the importance of trees.

Nebraska's first Arbor Day was an amazing success with more than a million trees planted that day. A second Arbor Day was held in 1884 and Nebraska made it a legal holiday in 1885, using April 22nd to coincide with Morton's birthday.

In the years following the first Arbor Day, Morton's idea spread beyond Nebraska with Kansas, Tennessee, Minnesota and Ohio all proclaiming their own Arbor Days. Today all 50 states celebrate Arbor Day although the dates may vary in keeping with the local climate. At the federal level, in 1970, President Richard Nixon proclaimed the last Friday in April as National Arbor Day. Arbor Day is also celebrated in other countries including Australia, Japan, Israel, Korea, Yugoslavia, Iceland, and India. Julius Morton would be proud. Sometimes one good idea can make a significant difference.

The Jewish holiday Tu B'Shvat, the new year for trees, is celebrated on the 15th day of the month of Shvat, which usually falls in January or February. It was originally based on the date used to calculate the age of fruit trees for the purpose of tithing as mandated in Leviticus, Chapter 19: 23-25. The holiday is now observed by the planting of trees.

The people who live in Israel today are very much aware of the importance of reforestation, the natural or intentional restocking of existing forests and woodlands. Throughout Bible history we find the forests and trees in Israel experienced extensive deforestation. Hebrew priests, ordered by Moses, used the bark of the Lebanon Cedar in circumcision and the treatment of leprosy. The Hebrew prophet Isaiah used the Cedar as a metaphor for the pride of the world. According to the Talmud, Jews once burned Lebanon Cedar wood on the Mount of Olives to celebrate the new year. King Solomon's Temple in Jerusalem and David's and Solomon's palaces used Lebanon Cedar in their construction.

Because of its significance, the word Cedar is mentioned 75 times in the Bible.

When the Babylonians under King Nebuchadnezzar conquered and burned Jerusalem, cedar although very beautiful and aromatic, burns very hot and fast due to the highly flammable resins in the wood so it added to the massive destruction of the temple and the city.

Sitting in a strategic crossroads between continents the Holy Land has served as a thorough-fare for advancing and retreating armies. History records more than 3000 years of War and violence in the land. Including the Israelite's assault on Jericho, the invasions by the Philistines, the Assyrians, the Greeks, the Romans, the Arabs, the Egyptians and even the Crusaders. Every act of War takes its toll on the forests and the woodlands of the country, often so drastically that it affects the ecology of the land to the point of changing the climate. Trees are one of man's best friends and their loss can be catastrophic.

A poem by Joyce Kilmer (1886-1918) expresses it succinctly:

I think that I shall never see
A poem as lovely as a tree.
A tree whose hungry mouth is pressed
Against the earth's sweet flowing breast;
A tree that looks at God all day,
And lifts her leafy arms to pray;
A tree that may in Summer wear
A nest of robins in her hair;
Upon whose bosom snow has lain;
Who intimately lives with rain.
Poems are made by fools like me,
But only God can make a tree.

Joyce Kilmer 1914

MOTHERS' DAY

Mother's Day is a holiday honoring mothers. It is not a religious holiday, per se, but it is celebrated in many locations around the world in an almost religious way. It is a day on which we honor our mothers. William M. Thackeray said. "**Mother** is the name for God on the lips and in the hearts of little children."

Mother's Day is celebrated on the 2nd Sunday of May in the United States and Canada. Mothers often receive special gifts on this day. According to the National Restaurant Association Mother's Day is one of the most popular days of the year to dine out at a restaurant.

I can remember my mother would announce to the family, **"Tomorrow the kitchen is closed . . . we will be eating out . . . it is Mother's Day.** That was my clue that she was taking the day off and we would be going to a restaurant.

Different countries celebrate Mother's Day on different days of the year because the holiday has a number of different origins. One idea is Mother's Day emerged from the custom of Mother worship in ancient Greece. The Greeks held a festival to **Cybele,** the great mother of Gods, in Greek mythology. She was the wife of **Coronus.** The festival was held around the time of the vernal-equinox.

In Rome, a festival honoring mothers was held from the **Ides of March** (March 15 to March 18). The Romans had another holiday, **Matronalia,** which was dedicated to **Juno.**

The United States copies Mother's Day from England and it was established after the Civil War by a lady named Julia Ward. Julia Ward was a social activist. Her mission was to unite all women against War. She is famous for having written the Mother's Day Proclamation.

In 1858 a young woman by the name of Ann Jarvis, who lived in Appalachia, organized women to work for improved sanitation conditions. She called her efforts **Mother's Work Days.**

In her memory, in some parts of the country, it is customary to plant tomatoes outdoors after Mother's Day. (But not before.)

In Proverbs 31:28 we find, *"Her children arise and call her blessed; her husband also, and he praises her."* **Amen**

HAVE A HAPPY AND BLESSED MOTHER'S DAY!

UNITED STATES ARMED FORCES DAY

Armed Forces Day is celebrated on the third Saturday in May, near the end of Armed Forces Week. Armed Forces Week begins on the second Saturday in May and extends to the third Sunday in May. The day was created in1949 to honor Americans serving in the five United States Military branches; **Army, Navy, Marines, Air Force and Coast Guard.** This was done following the consolidation of the military services into the Department of Defense. It was intended to replace the separate Army, Navy, Air Force, Marine Corp. and Coast Guard Days, but separate days are still being observed.

The first Armed Forces Days were celebrated by having parades, open houses, receptions and Air Shows. In 1962 President John F. Kennedy established Armed Forces Day as an official holiday to be conducted annually. The longest running Armed Forces Day celebration in the USA is sponsored by the city of Bremerton, WA. with a history of having conducted its parade since 1949, more than 64 years.

Due to the unique training schedules of the National Guard and other reserve units they are allowed to observe Armed Forces Day for their units at any time during the month of May. Armed Forces Day is not regarded as a federal holiday.

There are 47 other countries around the world who hold an Armed Forces Day which are celebrated at different times of the year to honor their respective military units.

> **"Speak softly but carry a big stick."**
> **Teddy Roosevelt**

MEMORIAL DAY

Memorial Day was originally called **Decoration Day**. It is a day of remembrance for those who have died in our nation's service. There are many stories as to its actual beginnings, with more than two dozen towns and cities throughout the USA claiming to be the birth place of **Memorial Day.**

There is evidence that there was an organized group of women from the South that were decorating graves even before the end of the Civil War. A hymn written in **1867** entitled. *"Kneel Where Our Loves Are Sleeping,"* by Nella L Sweet, credits the ladies of the South for decorating the graves of the fallen Confederate dead.

Memorial Day was officially proclaimed on **May 5, 1868** by General John Logan, National Commander of the Grand Army of the Republic. General Logan's *Order No. 11* was first observed on May 30, 1868 by placing flowers on the graves of both Union and Confederate soldiers at Arlington National Cemetery.

The first State to officially recognize the holiday was New York, in 1873. By 1890 it was recognized by all of the northern states. The southern states refused to acknowledge the day and continued to honor their dead on separate days until after World War I. When the holiday changed from honoring those who died fighting in the Civil War to honoring every **American** who died fighting in all wars.

Memorial Day is now celebrated, by almost every State, on the last Monday in May. A bill was enacted by Congress in **1971,** that made it a three day weekend and a Federal Holiday throughout the entire country.

In 1915, inspired by a poem *"In Flanders Fields",* by **John McCrae,** a young woman by the name of **Moina Michael,** wrote this verse:

> "We cherish too. The poppy red.
> That grows on fields where valor led,
> It seems to signal to the skies
> That blood of heroes never dies."

Moina Michael conceived an idea to wear red poppies on **Memorial Day,** in honor of those who died serving the nation during war. She was the first to wear a red poppy and sold poppies to her friends and co-workers. With the money that was raised going to benefit servicemen and their families who were in need.

Madam Guerin from France, visiting the United States, learned of this new custom and when she returned to France she began making artificial red poppies to raise money for war orphans and widows in her country. The tradition spread to other countries in Europe and by 1921 it had become a tradition. Madam Guerin approached the VFW with her plan and they became the first veteran's group to sell poppies nationally. The tradition continues to this day.

Traditional observances of **Memorial Day** has seemed to diminish over the years. Many Americans have forgotten the meaning of Memorial Day. At many cemeteries the graves of the fallen are increasingly ignored and neglected. Most people no longer remember the proper flag etiquette for the day. People look to Memorial Day as a three day weekend holiday. But there are still towns and cities that continue to hold Memorial Day parades and ceremonies. Our own Rhode Island Veterans Cemetery has a spectacular display of flags on Memorial Day. We should be proud of our heritage and keep it alive.

In 1951 the **Boy Scouts of America** began placing flags on the grave sites of the servicemen and women in our national cemeteries. The scouts from Troop 2 East Greenwich, place flags on each of the graves in the Rhode Island Veterans Cemetery. A great tribute to our veterans and an act of patriotism by the scouts.

What we need to do is to re-establish the solemn, sacred **spirit of Memorial Day.** Make it our traditional day of observance of our service men and women. The day that we honor our fallen heroes. In keeping with our **Memorial Day** celebration I would like to share with you the poem written by John McRae, entitled, "**In Flanders Fields**". The poem was written by a young Army surgeon who had witnessed the battle and carnage that took place in France at Flanders Field in World War I. It inspired him to write this poem that pays tribute to those who died. The verse admonishes us to never forget to continue to carry the torch and to keep the faith that those who died were not in vain.

In Flanders Fields

In Flanders Fields the poppies grow
Between the crosses, row on row.
That mark the place and in the sky.
The larks still bravely, singing fly,
Scarce heard amid the guns below.
We are the dead short days ago,
We lived, fell down, saw sunset glow.
Loved and were loved, and now we lie
In Flanders Fields.
Take up our quarrel with the foe;
To you from falling hands we throw,
The torch. Be yours to hold on high,
If we break the faith with us who die,
We shall not sleep, though poppies grow,
In Flanders Fields.

We need to acknowledge and praise God for having allowed us the freedom that we enjoy.

"May the Lord direct your hearts into God's love and Christ's perseverance."

2 Thessalonians 3: 15

Flag Folding Ceremony

The Uniformed Services Code, Flag Folding Ceremony, is a dramatic and uplifting way to honor the flag of the United States of America on special days like Memorial Day, Veterans Day, and at retirement ceremonies and funerals. Even as we fly the flag at our homes, our businesses, our churches and our schools we need to be steadfast in the way it is flown and know why it is requires such high respect and honor.

"The flag-folding ceremony represents the same religious principles on which our country was originally founded. The portion of the flag denoting honor is the canton of blue, containing the stars which represent the states of the Union. The field of blue dresses from left to right and is inverted when draped as a pall on a casket of a veteran who served our country in uniform."

At the ceremony of **Retreat** the flag is lowered slowly, folded in a triangle and kept under watch throughout the night, as a tribute to our nation's honored dead. The next morning it is brought out and at the ceremony of **Reveille**, it is run aloft quickly as a symbol of our belief in the resurrection of the body."

Folding of the flag is a very solemn and serious ceremony. It portrays the following:

The **first fold** of our flag is a *symbol of life.*

The **second fold** is the symbol of *our belief in eternal life.*

The **third fold** is made in honor and remembrance of the veterans departing our ranks who gave a portion of their life for the defense of our country to attain peace throughout the world.

The **fourth fold** represents our nature as American citizens trusting in God. It is to Him that we turn in times of peace as well as in times of War for His divine guidance.

The **fifth fold** is a tribute to our country for in the words of Stephen Decatur, "Our country dealing with other countries, may she always be right: but it is still our country right or wrong."

The **sixth fold** is for where our hearts lie. It is with our hearts that we pledge allegiance to the flag of the United States of America, and to the republic which it stands, one nation, under God, indivisible, with liberty and justice for all.

The **seventh fold** is the tribute to our Armed Forces, for it is through the Armed Forces that we protect our country and our flag against all her enemies, whether they are outside or within the boundaries of our republic.

The **eighth fold** is a tribute to the one who entered into the ***Valley of the shadow of death,*** that we might see the light of day, and to honor mothers for whom it flies on Mother's Day.

The **ninth fold** is a tribute to womanhood: for it has been through their faith, love, loyalty and devotion that the character of men and women who have made this country great have been molded.

The **tenth fold** is a tribute to fathers, for he too has given his sons and daughters for the defense of our country since they were first born.

The **eleventh fold**, in the eyes of a Hebrew citizen, represents the lower portion of the seal of King David and King Solomon, and glorifies, in their eyes, the God of Abraham, Isaac and Jacob.

The **twelfth fold,** in the eyes of a Christian citizen, represents an emblem of eternity, and glorifies in their eyes, God the Father, the Son, and the Holy Ghost. Amen!

When the flag is completely folded, the stars are uppermost, reminding us of our National motto, **"In God We Trust."**

After the flag is completely folded and tucked in, it takes on the appearance of a cocked hat, ever reminding us of the soldiers who served under George Washington, and the sailors and marines who served under Captain John Paul Jones, followed by their comrades and shipmates in the Armed Forces of the United States preserving for us the rights, privileges and freedom that we enjoy today.

Remember the white stripes on the flag signify purity and innocence.

The red stripes are for hardiness and valor. The blue field of honor signifies vigilance, perseverance and justice. The white stars are symbols of the states of the union.

HOW TO DISPLAY OUR FLAG

The American flag, when carried in procession with another flag should always be on the right—its own right.

Another flag or pennant may be flown above the American flag only during church services conducted at sea by a U.S. Navy Chaplain for Navy personnel.

When displayed with another flag in the crossed-staff format, the American flag should be on its own right—and in front of the other flag staff.

The U.S. flag should be centered and at the highest point when displayed on its staff with other flags.

When the American flag is suspended from a staff projecting horizontally from a building the union should be at the peak of the staff, except when the flag is at half-staff.

When displayed either horizontally or vertically against a wall, the union should be at the top and to your left. When in a window, the flag should be displayed in the same manner as seen from the street. During the unveiling of monuments or statues, the flag should never be used as a covering.

During the raising or lowering of the flag, or during its passage in a parade, all present should face the flag, and stand at attention with hand over their hearts. Men should remove their hats. Uniformed personnel render a right hand salute as the flag is raised or lowered and/or as it passes by.

When the National Anthem is played, all present should stand, face the flag with their hand over their hearts. Men should remove their hats. Persons in uniform should remain at attention, face the flag and salute.

Bunting for ceremonial or decorative use should be arranged with the blue on top, white in the middle and the red on the bottom.

When the flag is flown at half-staff, it should first be elevated quickly to the peak position, held there momentarily, and slowly lowered to half staff position. At day's end, the flag should be elevated to the peak position before lowering it.

It is the custom to display the flag only from sunrise to sunset, outside. However, the flag may be displayed 24 hours a day if properly illuminated during the period of darkness.

Fly the Flag long may it wave!

FATHER'S DAY

Father's Day, 2013, marks the 103nd anniversary of Father's Day. Have you ever wondered who started the Father's Day celebration and why it is so significant?

Although fathers have come a long way in a hundred plus years, some might say that they could likely use an image boost. Thanks to the antics of the of some of our movie stars, famous athletes, and political leaders dads need an image boost. Perhaps it is easy to take pop-shots at men who mess up, but it is important to focus on the role that men play in our 21st century society and empower them, make them more righteous and celebrate their achievements.

In 1908, in Spokane, Washington, a lady by the name of Sonora Dodd listened to the Pastor of her church, ramble on about the newly created Mother's Day and the importance of mothers. She told her pastor, "I liked everything you said about mothers and motherhood, but don't you think that fathers deserve a place in the sun, too?"

Sonora's father, William Smart, survived the Civil War and moved West to seek his fortune. His wife died in the winter of 1898 while giving birth to their sixth child. But Mr. Smart with the help of Sonora, the eldest child, the only girl, held the family together. She became convinced of the importance of her father and other fathers when at the time men were not considered very relevant to the family units.

It is obvious that William Smart made some unique sacrifices to keep his family together. It was tough and he worked very diligently at the task. But even in our own times, the 21st century, we are faced with some incredible challenges:

In these days 15% of single parents are men.
There were more than 158,000 stay-at-home Dads in 2009.

In 2011, 71 per cent of six year olds had breakfast and dinner with their dads. Many fathers are good about reading to their children and helping to raise them in a loving home.

At the other extreme. statistics report:

- 90 percent of homeless and runaway children are fatherless.
- 71 percent of high school drop outs do not have a father.
- 63 percent of young people who commit suicide come from fatherless homes.

A commentator recently wrote: "*Without concerned fathers, you would have no civilization.*"

Father's Day is hopefully a time when our culture says, "*This is our moment to look at our men and boys and recognize them for who they are. If we don't protect fathering, we will serve only to destroy our civilization.*"

Sonora Dodd certainly did her part to commemorate and promote father's day celebration. The first Father's Day was held in Spokane, Washington on June 20, 1910. Fathers in the church were honored by receiving a red rose, and people whose fathers were deceased wore white roses. Sonora Smart Dodd became the Mother of Father's Day. We owe a special tribute to her on Father's Day.

Let's give praise to all of our fathers. God our Almighty Father and all of the fathers on this glorious day.

Have a happy Father's Day

THE SEASONS SUMMER STARTS

It is the tilt of the Earth that causes the Sun to be higher in the sky during the months of June, July and August which increases the solar flux. Warm to hot temperatures prevail causing a lot of talk about "Global Warming." in the northern hemisphere.

By now you have had the lawn mower serviced, the garden planted and have made at least four trips to the beach. Depending on the price of gasoline at the pump, chances are you are making plans for a summer camping trip. In some parts of the country they are talking about special "seasons" loosely defined as the **tornado** season, the **thunderstorm** season or the **wildfire** season. Just keep your radio on and tuned to the weather station warnings and alerts.

Meteorological seasons are reckoned by temperature with Summer being the hottest quarter of the year. Seasonal weather fluctuations and changes depend on factors such as the proximity to oceans or other large bodies of water. That probably explains the reason for so many well-to-do folks from New York city having summer homes in Newport, R.I. Don't forget the excellent shopping and selective book stores.

> **"May they who love you be like the sun when is rises in its strength."**
>
> Judges 5:31 NIV

GRADUATION IS NO SNEEZE

June

June is the month for graduations and weddings. A graduate is defined as one who completes a college course of study and is presented with a sheepskin to cover his intellectual nakedness. The wedding or marriage, on the other hand, is defined as the greatest educational institution on earth. Graduations occur in grammar school, high school, junior college and university. but learning never stops. The diploma is often referred so as the "license to learn."

Proverbs 5: 1-2 reads:

> "My son, pay attention to my wisdom,
> Listen well to my words of insight.
> That you might maintain discretion
> And your lips may preserve knowledge."
> Proverbs 5: 1-2 NIV

The class of 2012 walked down the aisle in tandem. All four hundred ninety-two students filed into the already crowded auditorium filled with parents, grandparents, relatives, friends and neighbors. With their rich maroon robes flowing and their mortar-board caps they looked almost as grown up as they felt. It had been a tough course of study to reach their selected goals and the thrill and excitement of this moment was intense.

Dads swallowed hard behind broad smiles and mothers freely brushed away tears. Now they could begin to plan to spend some of the money that had gone for books and tuition. What a reprieve.

The class was seated on the platform. All was in order. But this class would **not pray** during the commencement exercises. Not by choice, but because of a recent court ruling prohibiting prayer in schools. The Chancellor and several students were careful to stay within the court's guidelines allowed by the ruling. Inspirational and challenging speeches were given but no one mentioned **divine guidance** and no one asked for **blessing**s on the graduates or their families. The speeches were nice. Well prepared and thought out, but they were somewhat routine until the final speaker was introduced. A young man came forward and he received a standing ovation. He smiled as he walked proudly to the microphone.

He stood still and silent for just a moment, and then it happened. All four hundred ninety-two students, every single one of them, suddenly **SNEEZED!**

The student on the stage simply looked at the audience and said, **"GOD BLESS YOU."**

He quickly walked off the stage as the audience exploded in applause, whistles and cheers. This graduating class had found a special and unique way to invoke God's blessing on their class and their future with or without the court's approval. This is a true story, it happened at the University of Maryland.

June is also called the wedding season. It is the most popular month for weddings and we can curiously ask the question, **Why?** The least popular month is January. I always wondered why couples choose November or December and then I thought perhaps it is because it is close to the end of the year and there may be some tax advantages.

There are many wonderful reasons to be married in June. The weather is usually lovely; the flowers are abundant; and June provides delicious seasonal foods like strawberries, melons, grapes, sweet corn, zucchini and tomatoes. Another reason for a June weddings might be that your mother was a bride in June or your sartorial tastes would like to have you float down the aisle in a chiffon wedding gown. The superstitious couple might like the idea of the goddess of June, **Juno**, smiling down on their wedding day bringing blessings to the bride and groom in their new life together. We all have heard this cute little rhyme that every bride knows:

> **Something old . . .**
> **Something new . . .**
> **Something borrowed . . .**
> **Something blue . . .**
> **And a sixpence for my shoe . . .** The last line often forgotten.

Something old, stands for the bride's life before her marriage.
Something new, stands for her new life with her husband.
Something borrowed, stands for the good luck that comes from borrowing from a friend.
Something blue tells of the color of the traditional wedding gown prior to the popularity of the white gowns that started in the Victorian era.
A sixpence for my shoe, symbolizes wealth.

> "Marriage is the high sea for which no compass has been invented. Marriage is a souvenir of love. Love is the river of life in this world. Think that you know it. Not until you have gone through the rocky gorge, and not lost the stream; not until you have gone through the meadow, and the stream has widened and deepened until the fleet could ride its bosom; not until beyond the meadows you come to the unfathomable ocean and pour your treasures into its depths—not until then can you know what love is."
>
> *Henry Ward Beecher*

"Love is patient, love is kind. It does not envy, it does not boast, it is not proud. It is not rude, it is not seeking, it is not angered, it keeps no record of wrongs. Love does not delight in evil but rejoices with the truth, it protects, always trusts, and always preserves. Love never fails." 1 Cor. 13: 4-6

JESUS ON THE 4ᵀᴴ OF JULY

We gather 'round to celebrate
   On Independence Day
Pay homage to our country
   As the children run and play.

With barbecues and picnics
   And fireworks in the air
The flag we own is proudly flown
   To show how much we care.

The stars and stripes spell freedom
   She waves upon the breeze
While bursts of colors can be seen
   Above the towering trees.

This is all quite wonderful
   We revel in delight
But God above in divine love
   Has brought this day to light.

With just a stroke of liberty
   A touch of His great hand
He gave democracy to us
   And helped this country stand.

The stripes upon our stately flag
   Were touched by His sweet grace
Each star of white that shines so bright
   Reflects His loving face.
So as you turn to face the flag

For battles that were fought
Be filled with pride for those who died
And freedom that they bought.

But don't forget to thank the One
Who gives the bright display
The reason why we paint the sky
On Independence Day.

Marilyn Ferguson ©2003
Used with Author's permission

INDEPENDENCE DAY

Pledge of Allegiance

Independence Day, commonly known as the **Fourth of July,** is a federal holiday in the United States commemorating that day in 1776 when the people of this land declared their independence from the King of Great Britain. Independence Day is commonly associated with fireworks, parades, barbecues, carnivals, fairs, picnics, concerts, baseball games, reunions and patriotic speeches.

During the American Revolution the legal separation of the Thirteen Colonies from Great Britain actually occurred on **July 2, 1776,** when the Continental Congress voted to approve a resolution that had been proposed earlier in June by Richard Henry Lee of Virginia.

After voting for **independence** the Congress turned its attention to the **Declaration of Independence a** document that explains their decision, which had been prepared by a committee of Five, with Thomas Jefferson as its principal author. Congress debated and revised the Declaration, several times, finally approving it on the **Fourth of July.**

There are many customs and traditions that can be recalled about the 4th of July, including some of the following:

- The observance that began in 1777 when thirteen gunshots were fired in salute in the morning and again in the evening at dusk on the 4th began in Bristol, Rhode Island.
- Philadelphia celebrated the first 4th of July in a manner with which we can identify. They had a dinner for the Continental Congress, complete with toasts 13-gun salutes, speeches, prayers, music, parades, troops passing in review, and of course, lots of fireworks.
- In 1778, General George Washington marked the day by declaring a double ration of rum for his soldiers and an artillery salute firing out over the Atlantic Ocean.

- In 1779, July 4th fell on a Sunday. The holiday was celebrated on Monday, July 5th. Now we celebrate Independence Day on the fourth of July regardless of the day of the week.
- In 1785 the Bristol, Rhode Island 4th of July parade began and it is the oldest continuous Independence Day celebration in the United States.

And we can go on and on recalling the notable events and occasions that we remember about the 4th of July. But, there is one account that I feel is important to share.

We may think that the **Pledge of Allegiance** does not fit with the theme of the Fourth of July. If so, you need to know this true story that will help you understand that it does.

Senator John McCain, Senator from Arizona and former candidate for the Presidency of the United States tells of his experience as a Navy pilot being shot down over North Vietnam in 1968:

"As you may know, I spent five and one half years as a prisoner of war during the Vietnam War. In the early years of our imprisonment the North Vietnamese Army kept us in strict confinement, but never more than two or three men to a cell.

In 1971 the NVA moved us from these conditions of isolation to larger rooms with as many as 30 to 40 men to a room. This was, as you can imagine, a wonderful change and was a direct result of the efforts of millions of Americans helping from home.

One of the men who moved into my room was a young man named Mike Christian. Mike came from a small town near Selma, Alabama. Mike didn't wear a pair of shoes until he was 13 years old. At age 17 he enlisted in the U.S. Navy. He advanced in his rank and earned a commission by going to Officer Cadet School. Then he became a Navy Flight Officer. He was shot down and captured in 1967.

Mike had a keen and deep appreciation for the opportunities this country and our military has for people who want to work and want to succeed. As part of the change in treatment, the Vietnamese allowed some prisoners to receive packages from home. In many of these packages were handkerchiefs, scarves and other items of clothing.

Mike got himself a bamboo needle, and over a period of several months he created an American flag and sewed it to the inside of his shirt. Every afternoon, before we had a bowl of soup, we would hang Mike's shirt on the wall of the cell and say the Pledge of Allegiance.

I know the Pledge of Allegiance may not seem the most important part of our day now, but I can assure you that in that stark cell block it was indeed the most important and meaningful event.

One day the Vietnamese searched our cell, as they did periodically and discovered Mike's shirt with the flag sewn inside, and removed it. That evening they returned, opened the door of the cell and for the benefit of all of us beat Mike Christian severely for the next couple of hours. Then, they opened the door of the cell and threw him in. We cleaned him up as well as we could.

The cell in which we lived had a concert slab in the middle on which we slept. Four naked light bulbs hung in each corner of the room. As I said, we tried to clean Mike up as well as we could. After the excitement died down, I looked in the corner of the room, and sitting there beneath that dim light bulb with a piece of red cloth, another shirt and his bamboo needle was my friend, Mike Christian. He was sitting there with his eyes almost shut from the beating he had received, making another American flag.

He was not making the flag because it made Mike Christian feel better. He was making that flag because he knew how important it was to be able to **Pledge Allegiance** to the flag of our country.

So as we say the **Pledge of Allegiance** we must never forget the sacrifice and courage that thousands of Americans have made to build our nation and promote freedom around the world. We must always remember our duty, our honor and our belief in our country."

"I pledge allegiance to the flag of the United States of America,
And to the republic for which it stands, one nation under God,
Indivisible, with liberty and justice for all."

RAMADAN

A Time of Spiritual Reflections and Prayer

Ramadan is the ninth month of the lunar Islamic calendar, which lasts 29 to 30 days according to the sightings of the crescent moon. It is the **Muslim** month of fasting in which Muslims refrain from eating, drinking and sexual relations. The rewards (*sawab*) are many, but during this month they are believed to be multiplied. Muslims fast in this particular month for the sake of demonstrating submission to God, and to offer additional prayers and recitations from the Quran, the Muslim Holy Book.

In Chapter 2, Revelation, 185 of the Quran it states that the month of Ramadan is that in which was revealed the Quran's guidance for mankind. It proves clear proof and guidance and establishes the criterion of right and wrong. It says that whosoever is present shall fast and whosoever is sick or on a journey Allah desires for them ease, He does not desire hardship and that you should complete the period and magnify Allah for having guided you and you should be thankful.

Thus, by the Quran, Muslims are informed that Muhammad first received revelations in the lunar month of Ramadan and establishes it as the most sacred month of all the months of the lunar Islamic calendar. Ramadan consists of three major practices: (1) **Fasting,** (2) **Increased prayer and recitation of the Quran,** and (3) **Charity.**

Ramadan is a time of spiritual reflection and worship. Muslims are expected to put more effort into following the teachings of Islam. One way of demonstrating their faith is the Muslim practice of **fasting**. Purity of both thoughts and actions is important. The act of fasting is said to redirect the heart away from worldly activities, the purpose being to cleanse the inner soul and free it from harm. It also teaches self-discipline, self control, sacrifice and empathy for those who are less fortunate.

In addition to fasting Muslims become **more prayerful** during Ramadan. They are encouraged to read the entire Quran. Some Muslims perform the recitation by means of special prayers called *Tarawith*, which are held in the mosques every night of the month. In a 30 day period the entire Quran is recited.

Charity is very important in Islam and even more so during Ramadan. *Zakat,* translated as "the poor-rate", is an obligation as one of the pillars of Islam. It is a fixed percentage required to be given by those who are able. *Sadaqa,* is a voluntary charity given above and beyond that which is required of *Zakat.* Muslims believe that all good deeds and charitable gifts are more handsomely rewarded during the month of Ramadan than any other time of the year. It is not uncommon to see people giving more food to the poor and homeless at this time. It is said that if a person helps a fasting person to break their fast, they will be rewarded without diminishing the reward the fasting person would receive.

Whether Muslim, or Christian, **"the righteous give without sparing."** Prov. 21:26

WHEAT AND WEEDS TOGETHER

August

When the month of August finally arrives we see a dramatic change in the vegetable gardens and flower gardens around our home. Depending on the daily temperatures, the amount of rain and how diligent we have been in keeping the gardens weeded, we will have a beautiful and enjoyable scene of colorful and exotic flowers, or a rather foreboding, depressing mess of weeds. Jesus challenges us when we read Matthew 13: 16-17 *"Blessed are your eyes because they see, and your ears because they hear." "For I tell you the truth, many prophets and righteous men longed to see what you see, but did not see it, and to hear what you hear but did not hear it."* *Matthew 13: 16-17.*

Then Jesus tells the parable of the sower. Remember the definition of a parable? An Earthly Story with a Heavenly Meaning. Jesus used parables as an effective way to teach and to make an everlasting point. Listen then to what the parable of the sower proclaims:

A farmer went out to sow his seed. As he was scattering the seed some fell along the path-way. The birds came and ate up the seed. Some fell on rocky places, where it did not have much soil and it sprang up quickly because the soil was shallow. But when the sun came out the plants were scorched and they withered because they had no roots. Other seed fell among the thorns which grew up and choked the plants. Still other seeds fell on good soil where it produced a bumper crop.

So what does that mean to us? How can we relate to this story? Jesus continues in the book of Matthew, verses 19-23, he explains with this story:

> *"When anyone hears the message about the kingdom and does not understand it, the evil one comes and snatches away what was sown in his heart. This is the seed sown along the path. The one who received the seed that fell on rocky places is the man who hears the word and at once receives it with*

joy. But because he has no roots, he lasts only a short time. When trouble or persecution comes because of the word, he quickly falls away. The one who received the seed that fell among the thorns is the man who hears the word, but worries of this life and the deceitfulness of wealth choke it making it unfruitful. But what was sown on good soil is the man who hears the word and understands it. He produces a crop yielding a hundred sixty or thirty times what was sown.

Matthew 13:19-23.

As we more fully understand the objective of the lesson we look out and see the gardens that we planted in the spring and wonder what we are to do. What about all those weeds?

Ralph Waldo Emerson defines a weed as, **"A plant whose virtues have not been discovered."**

Jesus told another parable. The parable of the weeds. He said:

"The Kingdom of heaven is like a man who sowed good seed in his field. But while everyone was sleeping, his enemy came and sowed weeds among the wheat, and went away. When the wheat sprouted and formed heads, then the weeds also appeared. The owner's servants came to him and said, "Sir didn't you sow good seed in your field? Where did the weeds come from? An enemy did this, he replied. The servants asked him, "Do you want us to go and pull them up?" "No," he answered, "Because while you are pulling the weeds you may root up the wheat with them. Let both grow together until harvest. At that time I will tell the harvesters: First collect the weeds and tie them in bundles to be burned. Then gather the wheat and bring it into my barn."

He who has ears, let him hear!

ROSH HASHANAH

The Feast of the Trumpets

If you are Jewish you know the meaning of this very important day, **Rosh Hashanah.** It is a day which occurs on the first and second day of Tishri. In the book of Leviticus we read: *"In the seventh month, on the first of the month, there shall be a Sabbath for you, a remembrance with Shofar blasts, a holy convocation."* **Leviticus 23: 22-23** This special day is also known as the Feast of the Trumpets. The rams horn or the **Shofar** was blown from morning until night.

Rosh Hashanah literally means, "head of the year" or "first of the year." It is known as the Jewish New Year. The name is somewhat deceptive, because there is little similarity between **Rosh Hashanah,** one of the holiest days of the year for the Jews, and our **New Year,** which sometimes consists of midnight drinking bashes and TV football games.

There is, however, one important similarity between the Jewish New Year and the American one. Many Americans use the New Year as a time to plan a better life, making resolutions, and new life promises. But, the Jewish New Year is a time to begin introspection, looking back at the mistakes of the past year and planning the changes to make in the year ahead.

No work is permitted on **Rosh Hashanah.** Much of the day is spent in the synagogue where regular daily liturgy is somewhat expanded. There is a special prayer book called the **Machzor,** which is read and the day is filled with prayer and reading from the holy book.

Another popular observance during this holiday is eating apples dipped in honey, symbolizing a wish for a sweet new year. Still another popular practice of the holiday is **Tashlikh** ("casting off"). The men walk to a flowing water, such as a creek or river on the afternoon of the first day and empty their pockets into the river, symbolically casting off their sins. We used to say, "They are shaking the lint out of their pockets." The religious services for the holiday focus on the concept of God's sovereignty.

Judaism has several different "new years" a concept which may seem strange at first, but consider this: American "new year" starts in January, but the new school terms start in September, and many businesses have "fiscal years" that start at various times. In Judaism, **Nisan 1** is the new year for the purpose of counting the reign of Kings and months on the calendar. **Elul 1** (in August) is the new year for the tithing of animals.

Shevat 15 (in February) is the new year for trees (determining when the first fruits can be eaten.) **Tishri 1** (**Rosh Hashanah**) is the new year for Sabbatical and Jubilee years. After the exile the day was observed by the public reading of the Law and by general rejoicing.

As Christians we are taught, and we realize, that we need to change and grow spiritually. We don't have to wait until a special holiday is declared, but then sometimes that helps. Christmas and Easter are special holidays that help us focus on our relationship with God and with each other. But, as Paul writes to the Romans:

> "*. . . we rejoice in the hope of the glory of God. Not only so, but we also rejoice in our sufferings, because we know that suffering produces perseverance; perseverance, character; and character, hope.*"
>
> *Romans 5: 2-4*

Paul suggests some basic things that we could do that would help to build our hopes:

1. We need to remember that our troubles did not take God by surprise. HE is still in control.
2. Believe that God has a solution, a provision, or a gift of wisdom to match our problem.
3. Pray, affirming our faith in God and expressing our confidence is HIS loving purpose for us.
4. Wait with expectancy and availability, trusting God to work out HIS perfect will.
5. Praise HIM—even before HE acts.

Happy New Year

LABOR DAY FOR THE LORD

Labor Day weekend is approaching. It is a National legal holiday that was established more than 100 years ago, in 1884. Over the years it has evolved from a purely **labor union celebration** into a general "last fling of summer" festival. Although it is not a religious holiday per se, we can see it as part of our Christian heritage as we recognize the working class of our nation. It also marks the time that many colleges, secondary and elementary school begin classes. A subtle blessing for all mothers who have endured their kids all summer long. And isn't it interesting that most of the children are ready to get back to school and see their classmates.

Labor Day is celebrated on the first Monday of September in the USA. Canada has its own Labor Day holiday. This year Labor Day is September 8th.

As a spiritual thought, we need to share some scripture that will bring bearing to this weekend holiday. The following scripture has application:

> "What does man gain from all of his labor at which he toils under the sun? Generations come and generations go, but the earth remains forever.
>
> The sun rises and the sun sets, and hurries back to where it rises. The wind blows to the south and turns to the north, round and round.
> It goes ever returning on its course.
>
> All streams flow into the sea, yet the sea is never full.
> To the place the streams come from, there they return again.
> All things are wearisome, more than one can say. The eye never has enough of seeing, nor the ear its fill of hearing.

What has been will be again, what has been done will be done again. There is nothing new under the sun, is there anything of which one can say, **Look! This is something new?** There is no remembrance of men of old, and even of those who are yet to come will be remembered by those who follow."

Ecclesiastes 1:3-11 NIV

These words found in Ecclesiastes are thought to have been written by King Solomon with his life largely behind him. He takes stock of the world as he has experienced it, between the horizons of birth and death. The latter horizon beyond which man cannot see. And, in spite of all of King Solomon's wisdom and experience he teaches us that God has ordered all things according to **His** purpose, and man should be patient and obey, enjoy life as God gives it. Man should know his own limitations and not vex himself. He should be prudent in everything, living carefully before God, protecting our environment, conserving our resources, respecting the things that God has provided, fearing God and keeping His commandments.

Of course being a Senior Citizen and having experienced various events in our lives we sometimes have a tendency to think that we have all of the answers, . . . and yet sometimes we only wished we did. Someone once said, **"Remember, once you get over the hill, you'll begin to pick up speed." And so it is.** Scripture teaches us that God won't give us more than we can endure. But then there are times when we wish that He didn't trust us quite so much.

King Solomon concludes his writings with this passage:

> Fear God and keep his commandments,
> God will bring every deed into judgment.
> Including every hidden thing,
> Whether it is good or evil.

Ecclesiastes 12: 134.

Love God and do as you please!

PATRIOT DAY

September 11

In the United States **Patriot Day** occurs on September 11 each year. It is a holiday designated in memory of the 2,977 men, women and children killed on that day in 2001 by the terrorist attacks made in this country. Initially, the day was called **Prayer and Remembrance Day** to honor all of the victims.

The U.S. House of Representatives Joint Resolution 71 was approved **by a vote of 407 to zero** on October 25. 2001. The Resolution requested that the President designate September 11 as **Patriot Day.** President George W. Bush signed the resolution in to Law on December 18, 2001 (as Public Law 107-89) It was a discretionary day of remembrance. On September 4, 2002, President Bush used his executive authority and proclaimed September 11, as **Patriot Day,** a day to be observed each year.

Patriot Day is not a designated governmental holiday. Banks and financial institutions remain open, schools and businesses are active, U.S. Postal Service is working.

On Patriot Day the American Flag and all other flags are to be flown at half-staff from dawn until sunset. The flag flying at the White House, the Capital Building, all U.S. Government buildings, U.S. Military bases worldwide and each American's home is flown in honor of the victims and their families. President Bush also asked all Americans to observe a moment of silence beginning at 8:46 A.M. (Eastern Daylight Time), the time that the first airliner struck the North Tower of the World Trade Center.

MAY GOD BLESS AMERICA!

YOM KIPPUR

Day of Atonement

Yom Kippur is known as the **Day of Atonement.** It is the holiest day of the year for the Jew. Its central themes are atonement and repentance. Jews traditionally observe this holy day with a 25 hour period of fasting and intensive prayer. They spend most of the day in the synagogue active in the various services. Yom Kippur completes the annual period known in Judaism as the **High Holy Days** or Yamim Nora'im (Days of Awe).

Yom Kippur is the tenth day of the month of Tisheri. According to Jewish tradition, God inscribes each person's fate for the coming year into a book, the **Book of Life**, on Rosh Hashanah, and waits until Yom Kippur to "seal" the verdict. During the High Holy Days or Days of Awe, a Jew tries to amend his behavior, to seek forgiveness for wrongs done against God and against other human beings.

The evening and day of Yom Kippur are set aside for public and private petitions and confessions of guilt. At the close of Yom Kippur one considers oneself absolved and forgiven by God. The Yom Kippur prayer services include several unique aspects: One is the actual number of prayer services held. On a regular day at the synagogue there are three times for prayer: (1) the evening prayer, (2) the morning prayer, and (3) the afternoon prayer. On the Shabbat, there are four prayer services. During Yom Kippur prayer services there are five prayer services. During the prayer services one must apologize to God and do the following:

1. Pray
2. Repent
3. Give to charity

As one of the most culturally significant holidays, Yom Kippur is observed by many secular Jews who may not observe other holidays. Many secular Jews will attend the synagogue on Yom Kippur because they consider the importance of High Holy Days and their need to be closer to God.

THE SEASONS FALL STARTS

The precise timing of seasons as viewed by astronomers is determined by the exact time of the transit of the sun over the tropics of Cancer and Capricorn for the solstices and the times of the sun's passing over the equator for the equinox. Solstice is defined as "the date when the sun reaches its highest or lowest point in the sky." The term equinox is "the time the sun crosses the equator making night and day equal in length."

Therefore, the following evidence is summarized:

> March 20 and September 22, 2013 the Sun crossed the equator making days and nights equal in time. (Equinox). This event starts the seasons of Spring and Fall.

> June 21 and December 21, 2013 mark the days that the Sun is is at its highest or lowest azimuth, thereby setting the beginning of Summer and Winter.

The real joy of the start of Fall (Autumn) is most of the yard work is done, except for raking the leaves, school has started, the temperatures are mild and the football season is well underway. It is a time to begin to view God's handiwork.

There is still the threat of an occasional thunderstorm with high winds and even a menacing hurricane. Keep a sharp look out for them.

"A prudent man sees danger."
Proverbs 22:3 NIV

DELIGHTS OF AUTUMN

I am a Jack O 'Lantern
My light will shine so bright.
For I am a Christian pumpkin
My symbols tell what's right.

My nose is like the rugged cross
On which the Savior died,
To set us free from strife and sin
We need no longer hide.

My mouth is like a giant fish
The whole wide world to show,
That Christians live in this house
And love their Savior so!

The story starts at Christmas
My eyes are like the star,
That shone on baby Jesus
And wise men saw from afar.

My color is a shiny orange
Just like the big bright sun,
That rose on Easter morning
Along with God's own Son.

And so when Autumn rolls around
Let's set our pumpkins out,
And tell the folks who see them
What God's love is all about.

Anonymous

COLUMBUS DAY

Columbus Day became a federal holiday in 1937, although people had celebrated Columbus' discovery of American and the Caribbean Islands since the colonial period. In 1792, New York City and many other U.S. cities celebrated the 300th anniversary of Columbus' landing in the New World in 1492. President Benjamin Harrison called upon the people of the U.S. to celebrate the 400th anniversary of the event. During that anniversary in 1892, teachers, preachers, poets and politicians used the event to teach ideals of patriotism and heritage. Framed around the subjects were themes in support for war, for citizenship, establishing boundaries, controlling immigration, the importance of loyalty to the nation and to God, and the awareness of social progress.

Catholic immigration in the mid-19th century induced discrimination from anti-immigration activists. Like other struggling groups, Catholics developed organizations to fight discrimination and to help the poor people. One such organization was known as the Knights of Columbus. They chose that name because they viewed Christopher Columbus as a fitting symbol representing the right to citizenship, as a Catholic, one of their own, and the man who had discovered America.

Many Italian-Americans observed Columbus Day as he was of their heritage. The first occasion was in New York City in 1866. In April 1934, as a result of lobbying by the Knights of Columbus, Congress and President Franklin Delano Roosevelt made October 12 a federal holiday. Since 1971 the holiday has been fixed to the second Monday in October. It is generally observed by the closing of banks, bond markets, the U.S. Post Office and other federal agencies. Most state agencies some businesses and most school districts close. The holiday nearly coincides with the birthday of the United States Navy (October 13, 1775.) Missed by one day. Both occasions are customarily observed by the Navy (and usually by the Marine Corps) by granting either a 72 or 96-hour liberty.

Not all States observe Columbus Day. Hawaii, Alaska and South Dakota do not recognize Columbus Day and abstain from celebrations. Hawaii has an alternate holiday called Discoverers Day. South Dakota recognizes a holiday known as Native American Day. Several other States have removed Columbus Day as a paid holiday for government workers but still recognize it as a legal holiday. They include California and Texas.

In 2007 several other State organizations have replaced Columbus Day with "Indigenous People's Day.

PUMPKIN TIME

Halloween

Paul writing to the Church of Colossae, in the New Testament Book of **Colossians,** expresses his concern because the young church that had been established by Epaphras and other converts of Paul, had become a target of heretical attacks and had suffered some serious problems in its growth. Paul doesn't go into great detail but he suggests that the heresy was diverse in nature and he makes a number of recommendations. In Colossians 3:2 he writes: *"Set your minds on things above, not on earthy things."*

Ceremonialism was one thing that Paul addressed. **Ceremonialism** held strict rules about the kinds of food and drink, religious festivals and even circumcision. Paul says, *"God has chosen to make known among the Gentiles the glorious riches of this mystery, which is Christ in you, the hope of glory. We proclaim him, admonishing and teaching everyone with all wisdom, so that we may present everyone perfect in Christ."* **Colossians 1:27-28**

One festival that we recognize today is **Halloween.** It is one of the oldest holidays with origins going back thousands of years. It has had an influence on many cultures over the centuries. It is known as **Pomona Day** by the Romans, **Festival of Samhain,** (pronounced sow-in) by the Celtics and the Christians called the holiday **All Saints** or **All Souls Day,** and later changed it to **Hallow Mass,** or **All Hallows.** It was celebrated with big bonfires, parades, people dressed up in costumes like angels and devils and included the carving of gourds, potatoes and squash.

Pumpkins are fruits, A pumpkin is a type of squash and is a member of the gourd family (Cucurbitacae) which also includes squash, cucumbers, gherkins and melons. The largest pumpkin pie ever baked was in 2005 and weighed 2,020 pounds. The largest pumpkin ever grown weighs 2009 pounds grown by Ron Wallace in Coventry, RI in September 2012. The pumpkin won the first prize of $5,500 at the pumpkin judging contest and was awarded a bonus of $10,000 for breaking the one ton record. Pumpkins have been grown in North America for more than 5000 years.

Pumpkins are low in calories, fat and sodium and high in fiber. They are a good source of Vitamin A, Vitamin B, potassium and iron. Pumpkin seeds should be planted between the last week in May and the middle of June. They take between 90 and 120 days to grow and are picked in October when they are bright orange in color. Their seeds can be saved to grow new pumpkins next year.

Pumpkin carving is a popular part of the modern American Halloween celebration. They can be found everywhere in the country from doorsteps to dinner tables. Despite the widespread carving that goes on every autumn, few Americans really know why or when the **Jack a Lantern** tradition began.

The practice of pumpkin carving originated from an Irish myth about a man nicknamed Stingy Jack. Stingy Jack invited the devil to have a drink with him. True to his name, Stingy Jack didn't want to pay for the drink so he convinced the Devil to turn himself into a coin that Jack could use to buy their drinks. Once the Devil did so, Jack decided to keep the money and put it into his pocket next to a silver cross which prevented the Devil from changing back into to his original form. Jack eventually freed the Devil under the condition that he would not bother him for one year and should Jack die he would not claim his soul. The next year Jack again tricked the Devil into climbing a tree to pick some fruit. When the Devil was up in the tree Jack carved a sign of the cross in the tree's trunk so that the Devil could not get down until he promised Jack not to bother him for ten more years.

Soon after that Jack died., as the legend goes, but God would not allow such an unsavory figure into heaven. The Devil, upset with the tricks Jack had played on him would not allow him into Hell. So, Jack had nowhere to go. The Devil sent Jack off into the dark night with only a burning coal to light his way. Jack put the coal into a carved out turnip and has been roaming the Earth ever since. The Irish began to refer to this ghostly figure as **"Jack of the Lantern"** and then simply **Jack O' Lantern.**

In Ireland and Scotland, people began to make their own versions of Jack's lantern carving scary faces in turnips or potatoes and placing them in the windows or near the doors to frighten away Stingy Jack and other evil spirits. In England large beets were used. Immigrants from these countries brought the tradition to the United States and found that pumpkins, native to America, make perfect Jack O' Lanterns.

Being a **Christian** is like being a pumpkin. God lifts you up—takes you in and washes all the dirt off of you. He opens you up, touches you deep inside and scoops out all the yucky stuff—including the seeds then lights your heart to shine.

Let your light shine for Jesus!

DAYLIGHT SAVINGS TIME

Fall

Daylight Savings Adjustment; the act of resetting your clocks from Daylight Time to Standard Time. It has taken from March to November to become acclimated to the hour you lost in the Spring. Consider that March 10 was a 23 hour day while November 3 will be a 25 hour day. But having that extra hour of light in the evening was great. Now get ready to rise in the dark.

The biggest problem in our house is to reprogram the clocks. Some clocks are simple while others require a review of the owner's manual to make the adjustment. I can still remember the Sunday we went to church and when we arrived there was no one there. What has happened? Did the preacher get sick or over sleep? Why hadn't the deacons prepared communion? It was great to get the first parking spot in the parking lot but there must be something wrong because the church has never been more vacant. Then someone else arrived and made a comment about Daylight Savings having ended. How foolish can one be?

As days shorten again in the Fall/winter sunrises get later and later meaning most people are waking up and spending a significant portion of their mornings in the dark.

During his time as an American envoy to France, Benjamin Franklin published a book of old English proverbs:

> **"Early to bed and early to rise, makes a man healthy, wealthy and wise."**

ALL SAINTS' DAY

The day for All Saints' Day varies from one church to another. Many denominations chose different days for this holiday. The holiday was thought to have begun as a festival of the Celtics, as a pagan holiday, celebrated in the spring. It was called the Feast of Samhain, (pronounced soween). It had as its theme the same rites celebrated by the Romans at their festival of Lemuria that is to exorcise the malevolent and fearful ghosts of the dead from their homes.

The festival of **All Saints' Day** begun in May, 610, by Pope Boniface IV when he consecrated the Pantheon in Rome to the Blessed Virgin Mary and all of the martyrs of Christianity. In the early 8th century Pope Gregory III proclaimed the holiday to include the relics of the holy apostles and all of the saints, martyrs and confessors who had been made perfect and are at rest throughout the world. The day for the holiday was moved to November 1st from May. It is now celebrated in November.

The festival continued after the Reformation of the calendar of the Anglican Church and in many Lutheran Churches. In the Church of Sweden (Lutheran) it s a role of General Commemoration of the Dead and is celebrated on the Saturday between October 31 and November 6. Some Lutheran Churches moved the date to the first Sunday in November. The Church of England celebrates **All Saints' Day** either on November 1 or on Sunday between October 30 and November 5.

Protestant Churches generally regard all true Christian believers as saints and if they celebrate **All Saints' Day** they use it to remember all Christians, both past and present. Other churches celebrate All Saints' Day on the first Sunday in November to remember not only those who have passed on but more specifically members of the local congregation.

ELECTION DAY

Be a patriot. Vote on Tuesday

Election Day is Tuesday, November 6, 2013. One of the most important responsibilities we have as Americans is to be involved in the electoral process. We have the freedom and the right under the Constitution to vote for those who are chosen to govern our country and guarantee our rights as declared under the Bill of Rights. We must carefully and prayerfully chose our leaders who are totally committed to the order of freedom.

Go to your polling place today and **VOTE**.

Remember this Proverb:

> **"When the righteous triumph there is elation, but when the wicked rise in power, men go into hiding."**
> **Proverb 28:12 NIV**

VETERANS DAY

November 11

Veterans Day was formerly known as **Armistice Day**. It is a United States of America holiday honoring the armed service veterans. The holiday is observed on November 11. It coincides with other days such as Armistice Day or Remembrance Day which are celebrated in other parts of the world and also mark the anniversary of the signing of the Armistice that ended World War I. This terrible war was thought to be the War that ended all Wars. Major hostilities of World War I were formally ended on the 11th hour of the 11th day of the 11th month of 1918, the time, date, month and year that the Germans signed the Armistice. Initially the holiday honored only WWI veterans.

Veterans Day is not to be confused with Memorial Day because it celebrates the service of U.S. Military veterans while Memorial Day is a holiday for remembering the men and woman who *died* in the service of their country. President Woodrow Wilson first proclaimed Armistice Day, November 11, 1919. In his speech President Wilson said:

> "To us in America, the reflections of Armistice Day will be filled with solemn pride in the heroism of those who died in this country's service and with gratitude for the victory, both because of the thing from which it has freed us and because of the opportunity it has given America to show her sympathy with peace and justice in the councils of the nation."

In 1945 following WWII veteran Raymond Weeks, from Alabama exposed an idea to expand Armistice Day to include all veterans not just those who died in World War I. President Eisenhower supported the idea of a National Veterans Day and in May 1954 a bill was enacted by Congress to change the name from Armistice Day to Veterans Day and it has been known as Veterans Day since.

Because Veterans Day is a federal holiday some American workers and many students have the day off. When Veterans Day falls on a Saturday then that Saturday or preceding Friday may be designated as a holiday. When it falls on a Sunday it is typically observed on the next Monday. Non-essential federal government offices are closed. No mail is delivered.

Veterans Day "Celebrate it at the appointed time."
Numbers 9: 3 NIV

HANUKKAH

Festival of Lights

Hanukkah is a Hebrew verb meaning "to dedicate", and is often Romanized as *Chanukah, Channuka* or *Khanukah,* It is known as the **Festival of Lights.** The festival is an eight-day Jewish holiday commemorating the re-dedication of the second Holy Temple in Jerusalem.

Judea was part of the Ptolemaic Kingdom until 200 BC, when the King of Syria defeated King Ptolemy V of Egypt, to take over Judea and make it part of the Seleucid Empire of Syria. King Antiochus III wanted to conciliate his new Jewish subjects so he guaranteed their right to "live according to their ancestral customs" and to continue to practice their religion in the Temple of Jerusalem.

In 175 BC, the King's son, Antiochus IV invaded Judea at the request of a group of Jews named Tobiads who wanted Antiochus IV to recapture Jerusalem. He complied marched on Jerusalem with a great army and took the city by force, slaying multitudes that favored the former Egyptian rulers. Antiochus IV ordered his soldiers to plunder, burn and destroy without mercy. He also spoiled the Temple, putting a stop to the practice of daily offerings and sacrifice of expiation. This lasted for three years and six months.

When the Temple in Jerusalem was looted and desecrated Judaism was outlawed in 167 BC. Antiochus even ordered an altar to Zeus erected in the Temple. He banned circumcision and provoked a large scale revolt.

The temple was liberated and rededicated. The festival **Hanukkah** was instituted to celebrate the event. Judah ordered the Temple to be cleansed, a new altar to be built and new holy vessels to be made. Olive oil was needed to fuel the menorah candles which were required to burn night and day. There was only enough olive oil to burn for one day, yet it burned for eight days, the time needed to prepare a fresh supply of oil for the menorah. As a result an eight day festival was declared by the Jewish sages to commemorate this miracle.

Hanukkah is celebrated by a series of rituals that are performed every day throughout the eight day period. Some are family-based and others are communal. There is no obligation to refrain from activities that are forbidden on the "Sabbath-like" holidays.

THANKSGIVING

Establishing a Memory

In the book of Ecclesiastes, in the Old Testament, we find some very important advice given to us by the writer, who scholars think was Solomon. The writer outlines a formula for a balanced life, or perhaps he tells us "What life is, not what it should be.

Chapter 3, verse 1, he begins by saying, "There is a time for everything, and a season for every activity under heaven." He continues and reminds us that there is a time for everything that we experience, from birth until death, from laughter to tears. He also reminds us that God has made everything beautiful.

"God has made everything beautiful in its time. He has also set eternity in the hearts of men; yet they cannot fathom what God has done from beginning to end. I know that there is nothing better for men than to be happy and do good while they live. That everyone may eat and drink, and find satisfaction in all of this toil—this is the gift of God." **Eccl. 3: 11-14**

We are fortunate to have a time established by our government to nationally thank the Lord for that which we have through God's bounty. We call that the time of Thanksgiving or Thanksgiving Day.

In 1621, after a hard and devastating first year in the New World, the Pilgrim's fall harvest was very successful and plentiful. There was corn, fruits, vegetables, along with fish, which were packed in salt, and meat that was smoke cured over fires. They found enough food to put away enough for the next winter. The Pilgrims had beaten the odds. They built homes in the wilderness, they raised enough crops to keep them alive during the coming winter, and they were at peace with their Indian neighbors.

Their Governor William Bradford, proclaimed a day of thanksgiving that was to be shared by all of the colonist and the neighboring native American Indians. Everyone was welcome and encourage to come. The custom of an annually celebrated thanksgiving held after the harvest continued through the years.

During the American Revolution (late 1770's) a day of national thanksgiving was suggested by the Continental Congress. In 1817, New York State adopted Thanksgiving as an annual custom. By the middle of the 19th century many other states also celebrated a Thanksgiving Day. President Abraham Lincoln proclaimed a national day of thanksgiving. Since that time each president has issued a Thanksgiving Day proclamation, usually designating the fourth Thursday of November as this special holiday.

In 1863, President Abraham Lincoln proclaimed a national day of Thanksgiving and since that time each President has issued a Thanksgiving proclamation, usually designating the fourth Thursday of November for this special day.

Now is the time for giving thanks. But how do we give thanks? The psalmist gives us some help, suggesting that we should:

> *"Shout for joy to the Lord, all the earth. Worship the Lord with gladness; come before Him with joyful songs. Know that the Lord is God. It is He who made us, and we are His. We are His people, the sheep of His pasture. Enter His gates with thanksgiving and praise His name. For the Lord is good and His love endures forever; His faithfulness continues through all generations."*
>
> *Ps. 100 NRV*

God likes to hear from us. We can talk with him at any time at any place and for as long as we want. We call it prayer.

Thank you Lord for all that we receive through your bounty, Amen!

BLACK FRIDAY

Black Friday is the day after Thanksgiving in the United States, and marks the time when the Christmas shopping season begins. On this day most major retailers open their stores extremely early, often at 4 a.m. or earlier. In 2011 several large stores including Target, Kohl's, Macy, Best Buy and Bealls opened at midnight for the first time. The stores offer very attractive promotional sales to entice the shoppers to come early and kick off the shopping season. Friday is not actually a holiday but some non-retail employers have been known to give their employees the day off, increasing the number of potential shoppers. Black Friday has routinely been the busiest shopping day of the year since 2005, although some reports claim it to be the busiest shopping day for a much longer period of time.

The day's name originated in Philadelphia, where it originally was used to describe the heavy and disruptive pedestrian and vehicular traffic which occurred on the day after Thanksgiving. Use of the term started before 1961 and began to see broader use outside the Philadelphia area by 1975. One explanation for the name was that "Black Friday" indicates the point in the year that retailers begin to turn a profit on their annual sales, or are finally "in the black". Many merchants objected to the use of such a negative term to describe one of the busiest and important shopping days of the year and claimed that their businesses had actually been profitable throughout the year.

Attempts have been made to re-name Black Friday, but they have been unsuccessful. Since the mid-2000s there have been reports of shoppers becoming unruly and assaulting other customers and store clerks during Black Friday sales. People who want to find a bargain or create a purchase will unfortunately resort to drastic measures.

ENJOY YOUR SHOPPING EXPERIENCE ON BLACK FRIDAY.

PEARL HARBOR DAY

December 7th

Pearl Harbor Day, the 7th of December. At dawn on Sunday December 7, 1941, more than seventy years ago, the naval aviation forces of the Empire of Japan attacked the United States Pacific Fleet center at Pearl Harbor, Hawaii and other military targets on the Island. The goal of the attack was to cripple the US Fleet so that Japan could attack and capture the Philippines and Indo-China and secure access to raw materials needed to support its military and economic power in Asia.

This would enable Japan to further extend its empire to include Australia, New Zealand, and India. The prevailing belief within the Japanese military and political establishment was that eventually Japan would control the East, Southeast and South Asia and the entire Pacific Ocean. The decision was made to proceed with the attack. Interestingly, Admiral Yamamoto, the Japanese naval officer who conceived and designed the Pearl Harbor attack, cautioned against a war with the United States. He had twice been a naval attaché at the Japanese embassy in Washington, D.C. and he knew the strengths and temperaments of the American people. He did not want to go to war with the United States. But he was overruled by his superiors and so he dedicated his efforts as Commander-in-Chief of the Imperial Fleet to a successful attack. Upon completion of the attack he was quoted as saying, "We have awakened a sleeping giant and have instilled in him a terrible resolve."

In the aftermath of the attack on Pearl Harbor there were many questions. How could an enemy like Japan impregnate and beat the defense system of the US Navy. Why would a small country like Japan dare attack a US Naval base? What happened to our military intelligence and Early Warning system? President Roosevelt and others within the government asked, "Why were our battleships tied side by side in the harbor?" This made them easy targets for the attacking Japanese planes.

We were complacent. But the reply was, "That's the way we've always done it."

Airfields, port facilities and warships were attacked and severely damaged. Of nine Pacific Fleet battleships at Pearl Harbor that day three were lost. The USS battleships Utah and Arizona were completely destroyed and the Oklahoma was salvaged but considered obsolete and was ultimately scrapped.

The Arizona lies on the bottom of the harbor and has been preserved as a tomb for its crew and a memorial to the events of this day. An observation structure has been built over the sunken hull and the ship's bell is appositely displayed in the center. At the end of the observation deck there is a marble wall with the names of the crew inscribed on it.

President Franklin D. Roosevelt made a speech to Congress the following day saying these words concerning Pearl Harbor. "Pearl Harbor, December 7, 1941, a date which will live in infamy . . . no matter how long it may take us to overcome this premeditated invasion, the American people in their righteous might will win through to absolute victory."

Pearl Harbor Remembrance Day is not a federal holiday. Government offices, schools, businesses, banks, and other organizations do not close. Public transit systems run on their regular schedules. Some organizations hold special events in memory of those killed or injured at Pearl Harbor. It is not a holy day for church goers but it is a memory that we cherish and hold dear to our hearts.

> Scripture: *"For everything that was written in the past was written to teach us, so that through endurance and encouragement of the Scriptures we might have hope."*
>
> Romans 15: 4

God created us as intelligent, artistic, creative, imaginative beings. How frustrating it must be to our Creator whenever we fail to fulfill our potential! It has been said that those who fail to learn from history are doomed to repeat its mistakes.

In Paul's letter to the Romans he gives us encouragement. Let's be sure not to fail to learn from God's book of history. Let us be reminded of the events of Pearl Harbor and learn from the mistakes that were made.

THE SEASONS WINTER STARTS

The Leaf-Peepers have all gone home. The Thanksgiving turkey has been eaten. Only remnants of Halloween trick-or-treaters candy remain in the bowls in the kitchen. Contenders for the Super Bowl are battling it out, and December 21 marks the official start of Winter.

It is very likely you have used the snow-blower at least once already and the car windshield ice scraper should probably be replaced if it to last till Spring. The major thing on the TO-DO List is to finish up the Christmas shopping, get the Christmas cards and letters in the mail and complete the decorating of the house and Christmas Tree.

Preparing for Christmas involves more than shopping, decorating, cooking and preparing for the holiday. It should include **Advent.** Christian churches celebrate a time of preparation for the coming of the birth of Jesus Christ. It is a time that is rich in tradition and laced with symbols reminding us of the coming of the Christ child. Advent is four weeks of lighting candles, counting the days, waiting with hopeful hearts for that sacred day.

The Advent Wreath is a popular tradition which traces its origin back to pre-Christian Germany and Scandinavia. People gathered to celebrate the return of the Sun after the winter solstice. The circular wreath made of evergreens had candles place in it. The wreath represented the circle of the year and the life that endures through the winter months. Candles were lighted to thank the Sun God for added light.

Lutherans in Eastern German were the ones who started the Advent Wreath as a Christmas religious custom. The first candle is lighted four Sundays before Christmas. The first candle is the **Hope** candle. It is purple in color. The second candle is the **Bethlehem** candle symbolizing the Christ child's cradle. It is also known as the **Love** candle. It is blue in color. The third candle is the **Shepherd's** candle and is also called the **Joy** candle. It is colored pink.

The fourth candle is the **Angels'** candle which represents the final coming. It is also known as the **Peace** candle. It is colored red. Finally, the last candle is the largest candle and it is placed in the center of the wreath. It is white, and known as the **Christ** candle. The **Christ** candle is always lighted on Christmas Eve.

We wish you a Merry Christmas and a Happy New Year.

THE SIGNIFICANCE OF CHRISTMAS

December 25th

Every time you look at your calendar or refer to a date, or write a date down you are using **Jesus Christ** as your reference point. The history of Jesus, is divided into two parts **BC** (*before Christ*) and **AD** (*anno Domini, in the year of the Lord*). Every other event in history and every event recorded on our calendar today is dated by how many days and years it has been since **Jesus** appeared on earth. Even your birthday is dated by *His* birthday. Then why shouldn't we celebrate His birthday?

When the angels announced the birth of Jesus to the shepherds keeping watch over their flocks near Bethlehem, the first Christmas night, they were promised that it would ***"bring great joy . . . for all the people.'*** For how many people? For all of the people. For some getting ready for Christmas it seems like more a hassle than a source of happiness. It is as source of stress and frustration. They feel pressure, not pleasure. It's a duty not a delight. They **endure** Christmas rather than enjoy it.

There are many possible reasons, you may feel uneasy. lonely or even depressed. You may dread spending time with oddball relatives. Maybe relationships are strained and uncomfortable in your family. Maybe you don't have anyone to be with this Christmas. Maybe you are confined and can't get out. Christmas may remind you of all of your losses or hurts or how things have changed. You may have a religious background that doesn't include Christmas, or you may have no faith at all. Watching others celebrate may make you feel uneasy. Maybe you are just exhausted and worn out from all that has happened to you life this past year.

This Christmas God cares most deeply about how you feel. Regardless of your background, religion, problems or circumstances, **Christmas** really is the best news you could get. Beneath all of the visible signs and sounds of Christmas there are some simple yet profound truths that can transform your life for the better here on earth to the forever in eternity. There is nothing more important for you to understand than the implications of Christmas in your life.

When we pause and consider the significance of Christmas we can receive and enjoy the best and most wonderful gift ever given. **It is God's Christmas gift to you.**

God's Christmas gift has three qualities that make it unique:

1. First, it is the **most expensive gift** you will ever receive. It is priceless. Jesus paid for it with His life.
2. Second, it is the only gift that you will receive that will last forever.
3. Finally, it is an extremely practical gift—one you will use every day for the rest of your life and you won't have to exchange it for color or size.

On the first Christmas night, the angels announced three purposes for the birth of Jesus Christ:

- *Christmas is a time for celebration!*
- *Christmas is a time for salvation.*
- *Christmas is a time for reconciliation.*

THE CHRISTMAS STORY   Luke 2: 1-20

"And it came to pass in those days, that there went out a decree from Caesar Augustus, that all the world should be taxed. And this taxing was first made when Quirinius was governor of Syria. And all went to be taxed, every one into his own city. And Joseph also went up from Galilee, out of the city of Nazareth, into Judaea, unto the city of David, which is called Bethlehem; (because he was of the house and lineage of David). To be taxed with Mary his exposed wife, being great with child. And so it was, that, while they were there, the days were accomplished that she should be delivered. And she brought forth her firstborn son, and wrapped him in swaddling clothes, and laid him in a manger; because there was no room for them in the inn. And there were in the same country shepherds abiding in the field, keeping watch over their flock my night. And lo, the angel of the Lord came upon them and the glory of the Lord shone round about them: and they were sore afraid. And the angel said unto them, 'Fear not: for behold I bring you good tiding of great joy, which shall be to all people. For unto you is born this day in the city of David a Savior, which is Christ the Lord. And this shall be a sign unto you; Ye shall find the babe wrapped in swaddling clothes, lying in a manger.

And suddenly, there was with the angel a multitude of the heavenly hosts praising God and saying, 'Glory to God in the highest and on earth peace, good will toward men'. And it came to pass, as the angels were gone away from them into heaven, the shepherds said one to another, 'Let us now go even unto Bethlehem and see this thing which is come to pass, which the Lord hath made known unto us.' And they came with haste, and found Mary and Joseph and the babe lying in a manger.

And when they had seen it, they made known abroad the saying which was told them concerning the child. And all they that heard it wondered at those things which were told them by the shepherds. But Mary kept all these things, and pondered them in her heart. the shepherds returned, glorifying and praising God for all the things that they had heard and seen, as it was told unto them. Amen" Luke 2: 1-20

CONTENTMENT

Paul writing to his disciple, Timothy, teaches

". . . there is great gain in godliness combined with contentment; for we brought nothing into the world, so that we can take nothing out of it, but if we have food and clothing, we will be content with these. But those who want to be rich fall into temptations and are trapped by many sense-less and harmful desires that plunge many people into ruin and destruction."

1 Timothy 6: 6-7

Josh Billings, an author, defines **contentment** as, "A kind of moral laziness." He goes on to explain: "If there was not anything but contentment in this world man wouldn't be any more successful than an angleworm."

On the other hand, do you have a compulsive need to find a solution to every problem and try to control everything? Do you always have a back-up plan in case things don't go your way? Have you noticed that the more you try to "fix" things, the more anxiety you experience? The Bible says, "The mind of the flesh [sense and reason] is death . . . But the mind of the Spirit is **Life**. Romans 8:6. Fixing is the opposite of "trusting." God does not want us to have total contentment. He wants us to live by faith and not by our personal desires.

God doesn't want us to be mindless or helpless, He just wants us to trust Him and live by faith. When we learn to trust God we will experience peace, even though we might be surrounded by tough circumstances.

One pitfall of human reasoning is that it causes us to be double-minded. That is to be unstable, unreliable and uncertain about everything. Must we always need to try to figure out everything? Why not try to be comfortable not knowing, and trust the One who does. Decide the next time you feel anxious about something stop and pray. Stop struggling with the **when,** the **where,** the **why,** and the **how,** and put your concerns in God's hands. then you will start experiencing God.

Begin your prayer by saying: **"Lord I am not going to try to figure this out myself. I'm bringing it to You, trusting You for the answer."** You will put yourself in a position where God can intervene on your behalf and help you. **Stop struggling and have contentment in Jesus Christ our Lord.**

A PENNY FOR YOUR THOUGHTS

We all probably have heard the usual stories of pennies on the side walk being good luck, gifts from angels **and so forth. In fact, as I was getting into my car today I looked down and saw a corroded little copper laying on the driveway. I stopped, reached down and picked it up, and recalled a story, told by a lady named Arlene.**

Several years ago Arlene and her husband Bill were invited to spend a weekend at the home of Bill's employer, Elmer Johnson. The boss was very wealthy with a fine home on a beautiful three acres overlooking the ocean. What a wonderful setting.

The first day and evening went well. Arlene was delighted to have this opportunity to see how the very rich live. Her husband's employer was quite generous and the perfect host. Arlene knew that she would never have the chance to indulge in this kind of extra special extravagant life style again, so she was enjoying herself immensely.

On the second evening of the visit, the host and his wife invited their guests to have dinner at an exclusive restaurant. Arlene had heard of this place but never dreamed she would be able to afford to have dinner there.

As the foursome were about to enter the restaurant, the boss and his wife were walking slightly ahead of Arlene and her husband. He stopped suddenly, looking down at the pavement for a moment. Arlene wondered what to do should she pass him? There was nothing on the ground except a small, darkened penny that someone had dropped, along with a few cigarette butts. Still silent, the man reached down and picked up the penny.

He held it up and smiled, then put the penny in his pocket as if he had found a great treasure. **How absurd!** What need did this man have for a single penny? Why would he even take the time to stop and pick it up?

Throughout dinner the entire scene nagged Arlene. Finally she could not stand it any longer. She casually mentioned that her daughter had a coin collection and asked if the penny he had found had been of some value. A smile crept across the boss's face and he reached into his pocket for the penny. He held it out to her to see. She had seen many pennies before.

What was the point? "Look at it," he said. "Read what it says." She read the words, **United States of America.** "No, not that. Read further." It looks like Latin, *E-Pluribus Unum,* which means "One from many." Read further, **One cent.** Right! "Now, turn the coin over and read the words above Lincoln's head," Mr. Johnson said. "IN GOD WE TRUST".

"Yes! And if I trust in the one God, **Jehovah,** the name of **God is holy,** even on this coin," he said, "Whenever I find a coin, I see that inscription. It is written on every single United States coin, and every bill, but we never seem to notice it. God drops a message right in front of me telling me to **trust Him.** Who am I to pass it by? When I see a coin I **pray.** I stop to see if my trust **IS** in God at that moment. I pick up the coin as a response to God, that I do trust Him. **I think it is God's way of starting a conversation with me. Lucky for me God is patient, and pennies are plentiful!**" Mr. Johnson remarked.

Psalm 37: 3-6 reads:

> Trust in the Lord and do good;
> dwell in the land and enjoy safe pasture.
> Delight yourself in the Lord;
> and he will give you the desires of your heart.
> Commit your way to the Lord; **trust** in Him
> and he will make your righteousness shine
> like the dawn, the justice of your cause like
> the noonday sun.

Whenever you find a coin, pick it up and read the inscription. Know that all of the things that have been worrying you and you have been fretting about, are things that you cannot change Read the message: **IN GOD WE TRUST,** and remember his promise: **Trust, Delight and Commit.**

THE TIME TO OBEY IS NOW

Scripture: **Luke 9: 57-63** says: *"Lord, I will follow you but let me first go and bid them farewell who are in my house."*

This was an occasion when Jesus was asking men to follow him. And listen to the excuses. Isn't it a shame, the excuses that we all give. **"I will do it in a minute . . . or first let me finish what I am doing . . . or** "I can't do it right now, but I will do it later."

I believe that most of us are familiar with these words. Unfortunately, our heavenly Father often receives a similar response. We have good intentions but we occasionally fall short. The Lord wants us **to obey now, not later.**

I'll never forget my **inner battle** one morning as I was mowing the yard, on my John Deere tractor. I was trying to keep a head of the dark clouds that were forming in the western sky. Boy! if I can only get this done before it starts to rain I thought. As I was mowing back and forth it suddenly occurred to me that I should be going to see my friend Jimmy. I can't explain why but it seemed that the Lord was telling me to stop what I was doing and go see my friend. As I continued mowing, the **inner feeling** began to feel more urgent. I'll go as soon as I finish this job. If I stop now it will be raining soon and I will never get it done.

How easy it is to make excuses when it seems to fit our wants. I promised the Lord that I would go over to Jimmy's house as soon as I was finished and had a chance to shower and clean up. **But,** somehow I knew that I should go right away. I shut down the mower just as the rain began. I went in and cleaned up and drove over to Jimmy's house. When I arrived I met Betty, Jimmy's wife, standing at the door, and she informed me that Jimmy had suffered a severe heart attack and had been transported by ambulance to Memorial Hospital.

She needed someone to take care of their two boys so that she could be with her husband. "How did you know that I needed you now?" she said. **I didn't, but God did.** My call from Him was made at the right time.

In **Luke 9: 67,** Jesus taught that some things can wait . . . they included mowing the lawn for me on that fateful day. The good news was that Jimmy survived his heart attack and recovered fully. The lesson is, **The Time to Obey Is Now. A ripe harvest cannot wait.**

> *Then in fellowship sweet, we will sit at His feet*
> *Or we'll walk by His side in the way.*
>
> *What He says we will do, where He sends we will go—*
> *Never fear, only trust and obey.*

In closing, I would like to share this story:

> Three boys were in the school yard bragging about their fathers. The first boy said, "My Dad scribbles a few words on a piece of paper, he calls it a poem and they give him $50."
>
> The second boy says, "That is nothing. My Dad scribbles a few words on a piece of paper, he calls it a song, and they give him $100."
>
> The third boys says, "I've got both of you beat. My Dad, is a Baptist Minister, he scribbles a few words on a piece of paper, he calls it a sermon, and it takes eight people to collect all the money."

DELAYED OBEDIENCE IS ONLY A STEP AWAY FROM DISOBEDIENCE

GOD IS WHERE LOVE IS

Meredith, a young lady of six, was grieving the death of her 14 year old black Lab. Even at six years of age, she could remember the wonderful times that she had spent with *Abbey* and she told her mother how much she missed her faithful friend. She was sad and would sit and cry because she couldn't understand. Finally, she asked her mother if they could write a letter to God so that when *Abbey* got to heaven God would recognize her. Her mother thought that would help so she wrote down the following words:

Dear God:

Will you please take care of my dog? Her name is Abbey. She died the other day and I know that she is in heaven with you. I miss her very much. I am happy that you let me have her as my dog, even though she got sick.

I hope that you will play with her. She likes to play with balls and swim in the lake. I am sending you a picture so that when you see her you will know that she is my dog. I really miss her.

Love,
Meredith

The mother put the letter in an envelope with a picture of *Abbey* and Meredith, and addressed it to *God-in-Heaven.* They put their return address on the letter. Then Meredith pasted several stamps on the front of the envelope because she said, **"It would take lots of stamps to get a letter all the way to heaven."**

That afternoon they dropped the letter into the letter box at the Post Office. Several days passed and Meredith asked her mother, **"Do you think God has gotten my letter yet?"** And the answer was, "I think He has."

A week later there was a package wrapped in gold paper on the front porch addressed to Meredith. It was in an unfamiliar hand writing.

Meredith opened the package and found a book by Mr. Rogers entitled, *"When a Pet Dies."* Taped to the inside front cover was the letter that Meredith had written to God. The envelope had been opened. On the opposite page was the picture of Meredith and her dog *Abbey* and this note:

Dear Meredith:

    Abbey arrived safely in heaven. Having the picture was a big help.

    I recognized *Abbey* right away. Ab*bey* isn't sick anymore. Her spirit is here with me just like it remains in your heart. *Abbey* loved being your dog. Since we don't need our bodies in heaven I don't have any pockets to keep your picture in, so I am sending it back to you with this little book for you to keep and have some-thing with which to remind you of her.

    Thank you for the beautiful letter and thank your mother for helping you to write it and sending it to me. What a wonderful mother you have. I picked her especially for you.

    I send my blessings every day and remember that I love you very much. By-the-way, I am easy to find, **I am wherever there is Love.**

God

Remember:

Happiness keeps you . . .	**Sweet.**
Trials keep you . . .	**Strong.**
Sorrows keep you . . .	**Human.**
Failures keep you . . .	**Humble.**
Success keeps you . . .	**Glowing.**

WHAT ARE YOU WORTH

If someone were to approach you and ask, "What Are You Worth?" What would you say? It might create more questions than answers. You might ask, "Do you mean what is my **net worth?**" If I take inventory of all of my assets, add up their value and subtract the sum of my liabilities what would my banker or my accountant say I was worth?

Ask your best friend the question. "What do you think I am worth?" You might be surprised at the answer. It might be an entirely different opinion than what you expected. Depending on how close you are with your friend, it may be very interesting.

What about your children? What do you think they would say if they were asked that question? You might get a whole different idea of your relationship with them.

Ask your boss or your supervisor the question, "What am I worth?" The answer would very likely relate to your job description and how well you performed. If you are in sales your worth might be reflected in the gross sales or revenues that you produce for the company. If you are an administrator the "worth" question would very likely depend on your professionalism, attitude and how well you did your job. How important are you to your company's profitability? A great deal I would trust. But certainly all of the answers are subjective. Doctor, Lawyer, Indian Chief, politician, parent or paper boy each has their measure of worth.

Ask your husband or wife, "What is my worth?" The answer might be very enlightening or even embarrassing. They might say, "You are worth the whole world to me," particularly when you mow the lawn, shovel the snow and take out the garbage, and by the way, I have been meaning to tell you, next time you take the trash out of the cellar don't forget the stack of papers next to the washer."

So we might conclude that our **Worth, or Value,** is directly related to and measured by the person or entity that knows us best. Perhaps at this time of year that might even include the IRS.

But more importantly, we might ask what is our worth to God? The Bible says that we are made in the image of God. ***"Then God said, "Let us make man in our image in our likeness and let them rule over the fish of the sea and the birds of the air, over the livestock, over the earth and over all of the creatures that move on the ground." Gen 1: 26 NIV***

So when we look at our worth through Christ's eyes, we see that He values us even though we are sinners. Why else would the Savior have died for us? There is **no room** for human pride or self love, every bit of our worth comes from God. God cares for us. He cares for **you**, He cares for **me**, and He cares for all the people on earth.

> Luke 12; 6-7. *"Are not five sparrows sold for two pennies? Yet not one of them is forgotten by God. Indeed, the very hairs of your head are all numbered. Don't be afraid; you are worth more than many sparrows."*

> Paul wrote, *"I have been crucified with Christ and I no longer live, but Christ lives in me. The life I live in the body, I live by faith in the Son of God who loved me and gave Himself for me."* **Galatians 5: 20.** His measureable sacrifice tells us that we are of great worth!

> His hands and feet and heart, all three,
> Were pierced for me on Calvary.
> And here and now, to Him I bring
> My hands, my feet, my heart. an offering.

The Death Of Christ is the measure of God's Love for us . . . and thereby establishes Our Worth.

RHUBARB

The origin of the plant named Rhubarb comes from the Greek. Rha, which was the ancient name of the Volga River along whose banks the plant grew wild. The word barbarous was added resulting in the name Rhubarb. It is described as a plant having long green and red stalks that are edible when sweetened and cooked until tender. It is also called the pie plant. Where the suffix word barbarous came from is unknown except that although the stalks are edible the leaves contain oxalic acid and can be very toxic. The leaves are poisonous.

Rhubarb generally is eaten as a fruit, but botanically it is classified a vegetable. Because of the tartness rhubarb is usually combined with a considerable amount of sugar. It makes delicious rhubarb sauce, jam and pies. Thus the name pie plant. In America a traditional flavor combination is rhubarb and strawberries. **In England,** rhubarb is mixed with ginger. The plant has a high amount of Vitamin A.

Another definition of **rhubarb,** in an informal sense is: **a quarrel, fight, or heated discussion.** We do know that this usage was popularized in baseball. The Oxford English-Dictionary has the first citation in 1943. Mr. Red Barber, sports-announcer for the Brooklyn Dodgers baseball team, used the term rhubarb to describe an argument or a mix up on the field of play. The word may also have had a connection with **"hey rube"** used to describe a circus brawl or an incident in the theatre.

In any event, I love rhubarb pie. Make it strawberry-rhubarb and that is even better. Or I would even settle for some rhubarb sauce. I don't know if it is the tartness or the sweet taste but it is good. Very good!

When we moved from Illinois to Connecticut, my father-in law insisted that we take a bushel basket of rhubarb roots to plant at our new home. When we arrived in Connecticut I carefully planted them in the garden anticipating a bumper crop. But I had no success. I tried for several years and finally, on my last try, the plants took root and we had beautiful rhubarb stalks growing next to our asparagus and tomato plants. I learned not to expect rhubarb to grow until the second year.

What I learned about rhubarb has provided me with several little object lessons:

1. *Rhubarb needs to go through a cold season in order to flourish.*

As Christians we need to go through cold times and times of trial in order to develop spiritually. In the scriptures we are consoled: "Consider in pure joy, my brothers, whenever you face trials of many kinds, because you know that testing of your faith develops perseverance."

James 1: 3

2. Rhubarb leaves are poisonous and need to be cut away from the stalk.

As a follower of Jesus certain things have to be cut away from our lives as we walk with Him. "Everyone who confesses the name of the Lord must turn away from wickedness."

2 Timothy 2: 19.

3. *For the best rhubarb desserts, you must add sugar or honey*

When we accept Christ, the Holy Spirit enters our hearts and because of His sweet presence added to our lives, we are changed as we bear the fruit of the Spirit.

"The fruit of the spirit is love, joy, peace, patience, kindness, goodness, faithfulness, gentleness and self control. Against such things there is no law."

Galatians 5:22-25 (NIV)

Dear loving creator, sustain me, cleanse me, change me. Amen

HAVE FAITH THERE ARE ANGELS

As we mature in our Christian faith, we sometimes wonder about whether **Angels** really do exist. We have been taught that there are **Angels.** We read about them in the scriptures. We know that the devil is a fallen angel. Perhaps you have wondered about how you would relate to an angel if you happen to encounter one. Then again, maybe you just haven't given it any thought to it at all.

As we read in Matthew 4: we learn about the temptation the Devil made to Jesus when he took him to the holy city and placed him on a pinnacle of the temple saying to him, *"If you are the Son of God, throw yourself down for it is written".*

> "He will command his angels concerning you, and they will lift you up in their hands, so that you will not strike your foot against the stone." Jesus answered him, "It is also written: Do not put the Lord your God to the test."

Mark gives us so hope that our guardian angel is looking after us, even we don't realize it all of the time. Jesus makes it very clear when he says:

> *"Have faith in God. I tell you the truth, if anyone says to this mountain. 'Go throw yourself into the sea: and does not doubt in his heart but believes that what he says will happen, it will be done for him. Therefore, I tell you that you have received it, and it will be yours. And when you stand praying, if you hold anything against anyone, forgive him, so that your Father in heaven may forgive your sins."*
> *Mark 11: 22-25.*

We are not here today to dispute or to prove the existence of angels. But we do say don't be surprised if you receive a blessing from one, even un-expectantly.

This story might illustrate the point. It is a story of two angels that were traveling through the land. It seems that the two decided to stop and spend the night, for they had grown weary in their long journey. The two angels chose to spend the night in the home of a wealthy family.

But the woman's family was rude and refused to let the angels stay in the mansion's guest room suite. Instead, the angels were given a small area in the cold, damp basement. As they made their beds on the hard floor, the older angel looked around and saw a hole in the basement wall and he quietly proceeded to repair it. "Why did you repair the hole in the wall?" Asked the younger angel. The reply was, "**Things aren't always what they seem.**"

The next night the pair came to rest at a house of a very poor, but most hospitable farmer and his wife. After sharing what little food they had, the couple let the angels sleep in their bed so that they could have a good night's rest.

When the sun came up the next morning they found the farmer and his wife in distress. The wife was in tears. Their only cow, whose milk had been their sole source of income, lay dead in the field.

The young angel was very unhappy and asked the older angel how he could have allowed this to happen. The first family had everything. They had a big beautiful mansion, lots of land and were very wealthy. They treated us very badly, and yet you helped them by fixing their wall.

The second family had very little but was willing to share everything, and you let their cow die. **Why? "Things aren't always what they seem,"** the older angel replied. "When we stayed in the basement of the mansion, I noticed there was gold stored in the hole in the wall. Since the owner was so obsessed with greed and unwilling to share his good fortune, I sealed the wall so he would not be able to find it."

"Then last night as we slept in the farmer's bed, the **Angel of Death** came for the farmer's wife. I gave him the cow instead." **Things aren't always what they seem.**

Sometimes that is exactly what happens when things don't turn out the way we think they should. If you have **Faith,** you just need to trust that every outcome is always to your advantage. *You just might not know it until sometime later.*

Have Faith and Believe

THE WORD

The English language has a number of wonderfully anthropomorphic collective-nouns that are used to identify different groups of animals, birds, fish, and other species that we know. As an example, they might include the following:

We are all familiar with terms like a Team of-horses; A Kin of cows; a Brood of chickens; a Herd of rabbits; a School of fish. You may have even used the collective-noun a Gaggle of geese or a Tribe of goats, We all are familiar with the term a Pack of wolves.

However, less widely known nouns might include: A Pride of lions; a Murder of crows or ravens. What about an Exaltation of Doves or an Aerie of Eagles. And there is a Bask of crocodiles, a Clowder of cats and a Kennel of dogs. Some collective-nouns make sense, others defy logic. A Crash of rhinos, a Pickle of porcupines, a Rafter of turkeys, a Labor of moles, a Bed of oysters and a Pod of porpoises. We also may find an Army of caterpillars and a Coalition of cheetahs.

But consider the baboon. They are the loudest, the most dangerous, the most obnoxious and most vicious, aggressive and least intelligent of all the primates. The proper collective-noun for a group of baboons is . . . **a Congress.** I guess that pretty well explains the things that are coming out of Washington, D.C. these days. Another animal group that you might wish to consider is: a Nag of wives, or a Jerk of husbands.

"Colors fade, temples crumble, empires fall but wise words endure." *Edward Thorndike.*

An author once wrote this definition of words: "We could have a great many fewer disputes in the world if words were taken for what they are . . . the signs of our ideas only, and not for things themselves." *John Locke.*

When we open our Bibles we find that the writers of the scriptures, blessed by God, reveal another definition of "The Word." Romans 10: 8 presents another synoptic view. Paul writing to the church in Rome proclaims: "The word is near you, on your lips and in your heart, that is, the word of faith we are proclaiming. That if you confess with your mouth

"Jesus is Lord," and believe in your heart that God raised Jesus from the dead, you will be saved. For it is with your heart that you believe and are justified, and it is with your mouth that you confess and are saved."

As the scripture says, "Anyone who trusts in him will never be put to shame.' For there is no difference between Jew and Gentile—the same Lord is Lord of all and richly blesses all who call upon him. For Everyone who calls on the name of the Lord will be saved." NIV.

Don't wait for something big to occur. Start where you are, with what you have, and that will always lead you into something greater. The person who moves mountains begins by carrying away small stones.

FORTY A ROUND NUMBER

From early times certain numbers and their multiples have been chosen as **special** numbers because they were thought to have a sacred or symbolic significance. Ancient Rabbis developed the theory that all numbers have a secret meaning.

The numbers **3, 4, 7, 10, 12, 40, and 70,** were deemed to be sacred numbers and were used conventionally and symbolically. As we read and study the Bible we discover this to be true. For example; the number **3** expressed **emphasis**, as in *"I will overturn, overturn, overturn it."* Ezek 21:27. From early times the number 7 was considered **sacred** among the Semites and is believed to be the **perfect number**. The number **10** was regarded as a **complete number.**

In the book of Revelation there is reference to the **Beast of The World,** when we read about it in Chapter 13: 18, it says, *"This calls for wisdom. If anyone has insight, let him calculate the number of the beast, for it is man's number. The number is 666."* There are various schemes for decoding that number but the popular one is that **666** is the symbol of the trinity of evil and imperfection—each digit falls short of the perfect number **7.**

The number **40** is considered to be a **round number**. That is the number **40** is used to describe the period from the beginning to the end. In Exodus 24:18 we read, *"Moses stayed on Mt. Sinai for 40 days and 40 nights."* while he met with God.

1 Kings 19:8 tells of Elijah and how he had to flee for his life. He was exhausted and without hope when two angels came and offered him something to eat. He got up and ate and drank. Strengthened by the food he was able to travel for forty days and forty nights until he reached **Mt. Horeb,** God's mountain.

In Genesis there are four chapters that reveal the greatest catastrophe ever experienced on earth. **The Great Flood.** Noah was chosen by God to build an Ark and God told Noah to load pairs of clean and unclean animals, birds and creatures aboard the Ark. He told Noah to take his wife and their three sons and their wives and get on board. When Noah had finished it began to rain and it rained for **40 days and 40 nights,** until the waters covered the land and the mountains to a depth of more than twelve feet. All of the people and creatures who remained on the earth perished. The water covered the earth for a hundred and fifty days.

2 Samuel 5:4 tells of David who was thirty years of age when he became King of Israel and reigned for **40 years. Exodus 16:35** tells the story of Moses who led the Israelites out of bondage in Egypt only to wander through the wilderness for **40 years.** God provided for them by giving them manna to eat.

Life begins at forty. A person who is **Forty** is a quadragenarian. **Forty** is the *old age* of youth, while **Fifty** is the *youth* of old age. **Forty** is the age a woman says she is when she is **50. And So It Is.**

Can you remember what you were doing **40 years** ago? That was 1971. I remember that I had moved my wife, five kids and a pregnant mini-schnauzer from Denver, Colorado to Bloomfield, Connecticut and that started a new era in my life.

In the spirit of numerology I submit the following numbers: **40, 10, 7, 12, 1 and 3.** in recognition of Mary Ostiguy, from the First Baptist Church in Wickford for the work she has done in developing the nursing home ministries in Rhode Island for more than forty years.

Explanation:

40   is the round-number for her work, from beginning to the end.

10   is the complete number for her total commitment to this program.

7   is the perfect number for the perfect job she has done.

12   is the disciples' number for her unselfishness and thoughtful commitment.

1   is the special number for one beloved person—Mary Ostiguy.

3   expresses and emphasizes the appreciation that we have for her.

PROCRASTINATION

Procrastination is a "Five-Dollar" word. Or at least it is a five-syllable word, which is defined as a word that has five parts, uttered by one short effort. (Pro-kras-ti-na-tion) One writer defines the word as, "*The art of keeping up with yesterday.*" The dictionary defines procrastination as "putting off action, or slow to act." And yet another writer says simply. "*It is a thief of time.*"

Most everybody procrastinates. If you consider yourself a procrastinator you are not alone. We all do it, some may do it more than others. The fact that you procrastinate doesn't mean that you lack intelligence or that you are lazy. Procrastination is a **habit,** and a habit that we can easily overcome.

Why do we procrastinate? Research has shown that those who do tend to do this seem to be self-critical. So, as you consider your "putting off till tomorrow" habit by developing differ—rent work or action demeanor, try to be gentle on yourself. Punishing yourself every time you become aware of the fact that you postponed something isn't going to change you for the better Rewarding yourself when you make progress will.

Procrastinating can be very costly in many ways:

- It may be costly to your health. Dr. Joseph Ferrari, PhD. reported that during one semester at the University where he teaches, procrastinating students had more colds, suffer more from the flu and experienced more gastrointestinal problems and bouts of insomnia than their non-procrastinating peers.
- Procrastinating has a high cost to others as well as yourself. It forces others to take on additional responsibilities, and those impacted became resentful. It puts a strain on teamwork and on personal relationships in the home and the workplace.
- Procrastination can also damage you financially. How many of you have written a check for a bill you received and then put off mailing it because you were running a little short that month?

Whoops! Now next month you have a $35.00 late charge on your account because the letter didn't get posted on time. You don't need that expense.

- A survey of H & R Block, found that waiting until the last minute to file taxes cost people an average of $400 because of the errors that are made trying to get the report in at the last minute. The Block report said that the errors that were made totaled $473 million dollars in over-payment in 2011. Consider how much money you could save on gifts by buying them when they are on sale. And the time you can save by not searching store after store at the last minute, after everything has been picked over. Of course the trick is to put that gift away in a safe place so you will remember where it is when the time comes.

- We also put things off to distract ourselves as a way of regulating our emotions, such as fear of failure. Procrastinators actively look for distractions, particularly ones that don't require a lot of commitment on their part.

- Have you ever put off shoveling the snow from the walk because you needed to finish reading the last chapter of your home-work assignment. Remember what happened? The puffy white stuff started to melt, then turned to ice and finally became a solid sheet that couldn't be moved.

- Or, perhaps you went to the laundry room and looked at the mound of ironing that seemed to tower over your head like a great monolith. You simply turned and said, "It is too big to contemplate, so I think I will go to my friend Jane's house and see how she is doing. This can wait until tomorrow. In the book of James, chapter 4:13 we read some good advice scripturally. Remember James was a brother of Jesus, thought to have been the oldest brother, and James' epistle was written to the members of the twelve Jewish tribes scattered throughout the nation of Israel. James' letter was meant for the Jewish believers but has sound advice for Christians.

In Chapter 4:13 James is boasting about tomorrow.

"Today or tomorrow we will go to this or that city, spend a year there carry on business and make money. Why you don't even know

*what will happen tomorrow. What is your life? You are a mist that appears for a little while and then vanishes. Instead you ought to say, 'If it is the Lord's will, we will live and do this or that.' As it is, you boast and brag. All such boasting is evil. Anyone who knows the good he ought to do and doesn't do it, **Sins.** "*

Being happy doesn't mean everything is perfect. It means you've decided to see beyond the imperfection. Begin by eliminating procrastination.

NO CHARGE FOR LOVE

"The steadfast love of the LORD never ceases, his mercies never come to an end; they are new every morning; great is your faithfulness."
                                                Lamentations 3: 22-23 (NISV)

How often do we hear the word LOVE used? What does it mean? We have all heard people say, "I just love your new dress." or, "Don't you simply love that new book? Or how often do we say, "I LOVE You," to our spouse, our children or our friends? One needs to stop and ask, "What do we mean when we use this expression?

One person said, "LOVE is like the measles, we can have it only once, and the later in life we have it, the tougher it is on us."

William Penn said, "Knowing LOVE is the hardest lesson in Christianity; but for that reason it should be our most important consideration in learning."

The Book of John is one of the four Gospels, but is noticeably different than the other three, Matthew, Mark and Luke. The Book of John is known as the LOVE Gospel and makes many references to the word LOVE. Perhaps the most memorable is John 3:16, *"For God so loved the world that he gave his only son that whoever believes in him shall not perish but have eternal life." (NIV).*

One of the best ways to teach a lesson is to use a story as an example:

A farmer had some puppies he wanted to sell. He painted a sign advertising the puppies and set about nailing it to a post at the end of his lane. As he was hammering the last nail into the post he felt a tug on his overalls. He looked around and into the eyes of a little boy.

"Mister," the boy said, "I want to buy one of your puppies."

"Well." said the farmer, as he rubbed the sweat off the back of his neck, "These puppies are pretty special, they come from very fine parents and they cost a good deal of money."

The boy dropped his head for a moment, then reaching deep into his pocket, he pulled out a handful of change and held it up to the farmer. I've got thirty-nine cents. Is that enough to take a look?"

"Sure," said the farmer. With that he invited the boy to take a walk up to the barn. As they approached the barn the farmer whistled, "Here Molly!" he called. Out from the barn came the mother dog, Molly, followed by four little balls of fur. The little boy pressed his face against the chain-link fence. His eyes were like saucers and they danced with delight. As the puppies made their way towards the fence, the little boy noticed something else stirring inside the barn.

Slowly another little ball of fur appeared, this one noticeably smaller. Out of the barn it came, but in a somewhat awkward manner. The little pup began hobbling toward the others, doing its best to catch up.

"I want that one," the little boy said, pointing to the runt. The farmer knelt down at the boy's side and said, "Son, you don't want that puppy. He will never be able to run and play with you like these other dogs would."

With that the little boy stepped back from the fence, reached down and began rolling up one leg of his trousers. In doing so he revealed a steel brace running down both sides of his leg attaching itself to a specially made shoe.

Looking back up at the farmer, he said, "You see sir, I don't run too well myself, and that puppy will need someone who understands."

With tears in his eyes, the farmer reached down and picked up the little pup. Holding it carefully he handed it to the little boy.

"How much?" asked the little boy . . . "No charge," answered the farmer. "There is NO CHARGE FOR LOVE."

When and where have we not said Yes to God?

A SEASON FOR EVERTHING

When I was growing up in Springfield, Illinois, we had the most beautiful sugar maple tree in our front yard. My father had planted the tree on Arbor Day years earlier, with great ceremony, and he told us to watch it grow as we matured. It was his pride and joy. Each fall its leaves would burst forth with the most beautiful array of colors. Finally, when the colors were full he would remind us, at breakfast, "Don't forget to notice how beautiful the maple tree is today. It won't be that way very long. Enjoy them before your bus comes."

I was always glad that Dad had reminded us to take a moment to notice the tree's brilliant colors, otherwise I probably would have dashed off to school without even seeing the beauty God had provided. Why is it that we seem to take so many things for granted and miss so much of what we have?

When we moved the family from Colorado to Connecticut we became very much aware of the differences of the autumn season. Certainly, Colorado has some spectacular colors and when you go to the mountains and see the Aspen trees with their fall colors on display it is breath taking. It seems as though God has spread French's Mustard over the mountain side because they turn a beautiful yellow mustard color in appearance.

But make no mistake. There is nothing like the colors displayed in New England in the fall. With the spectacular colors all around, we would take drives through the country side to see the colors change. I still get excited when I see how fall comes upon us so quickly in this area and almost shouts to us of the beauty God has created for our enjoyment.

Autumn in New England offers us a panorama of shades of red, yellow, green, and orange. Everything seems to remind us that **life is good.**

The author of Ecclesiastes reminds us that there is a season and time for **everything.** Some of us are now in what is called the autumn season of our lives. What a beautiful time this can be. Sometimes we forget to notice the beauty and instead focus on how **"bare the limbs have become."**

It happens, and how easy it is to over look the beauty of the trees and focus on the empty limbs.

This autumn I challenge you to look at the colors that God has placed in the **leaves of our lives. Praise the Lord for how beautiful our lives have become over time.**

> *Prayer:* ***Thank you Lord for this beautiful day that you have given to each of us. Thank you for the beauty that you have created, and for the beauty of Your presence. Surround us with your love as we rejoice in Jesus' name.***
> ***Amen***

ANOTHER NEW YEAR

"Now you are the body of Christ, and each one of you is a part of it."
1 Corinthians 12:27 NIV

This year at the First Baptist Church East Greenwich, we were blessed by the children of the church. Under the direction of Donna O'Brien the church's Director of Music and choir director and Rebekah Malone, the pastor's wife, we were sanctified to hear several beautiful Christmas melodies played by the Children's Hand-Bell Choir. I had a deep sense that God wanted me to learn something from this experience. The presentations were absolutely beautiful. Each bell-ringer was intent to play his or her bell at the proper time. Even if one person failed, it would result in the failure of continuity and rhythm of the song which would be affected, we would lose the beauty of the music. Bells played incorrectly can create discordant chords and change the melody. Not a single person is unimportant or unnecessary in a Bell-Ringer Choir. For the listeners to hear the music and appreciate the message in song, each bell-ringer had to ring his or her bell on cue. I am proud and pleased to tell you that the Bell-ringers were perfect.

It occurred to me there is an a lesson to be learned from this example. Each of us has a unique part to play in the melody of life which God has orchestrated for us. If we fail to do our part or play the wrong rhythm the melody will be hindered in significant ways. Souls will not be reached. Others may not be nourished. Some may fall by the wayside. The melody and the message may not be received if we choose to play a tune of our own making. Only as each of us follow our Heavenly Father will the melody be complete and be beautiful.

New Year's Eve has come and gone. Now we are destined to face the challenges and adventures that lie ahead in the year 2013. Some folks I know, do not look forward to the new year with great anticipation. Others are filled with enthusiasm and expectancy. I was thinking about the future and what is ahead and I was reminded of a unique New Year's Eve party I had once attended. The affair was held at a friend's large beautiful home located on a magnificent lakeshore. The view was breathtaking. The moon was bright and the stars twinkled in the dark sky.

The room we were in was a large, beautifully decorated room. Two large tables were filled with snacks and desserts. There was a lot of laughter and good will as we played several games. Finally, the host announced, as we approached the midnight hour, we would play a final game called **Resolution.** Each person was given a slip of paper and was told to complete this sentence: ***"This year I will try to . . ."*** When we were finished the host gathered up the papers and started to read them aloud:

> "I will try to lose ten pounds."
> "I will try to be on time for my appointments."
> "I will try to keep within my budget."

There was much laughter as we tried to guess who had written each resolution. Then came one which stopped all of the laughter and started some serious thinking:

> "I will try to love the unlovely."

After a brief silence I heard, "It is a wonderful resolution." "Why don't we all try it?" Quite a discussion followed, and we each agreed to give this one a try. Some mentioned specific things they could do in the coming months. Others recalled times in the past when they failed to show love or kindness and how it could be changed.

During the exchange of ideas the clock chimed midnight and it was time for kisses and noise makers. A new year had arrived. The fun continued but when it came time to go home I believe many went home with a new resolution and with a determination to give it a try. I know I did!

It is never too late to make a new year's resolution, or to replace the one you haven't kept. "Try to love the unlovely. Jesus did."

> *"Accept one another, then, just as Christ accepted you in order to bring praise to God."*
>
> Romans 15:7 NIV

A CUP OF COFFEE

Scripture: *"Better a dry crust with peace and quiet than a house full of feasting with strife."*

Proverb 17:1

Having raised five children, two girls and three boys, I could relate to this scripture very easily. Sometimes I would have preferred that my wife had fed the kids earlier so that the two of us could sit down and spend a quiet time together talking about the events of the day without a lot of strife.

Strife is defined as: **"a conflict or struggle between opposed persons or things."** And so it is at times, even with our own children.

Perhaps this story may better illustrate the point: A group of college graduates from a nearby university had gathered together to talk about their careers, what they had been doing and how their lives had changed from the time that they had been in school.

They decided to go visit their old university teacher, Professor Ed Johnson, who was retired but had always been an inspiration to each of them. During their visit the conversation turned to complaints about stress, the pressures of life; their work, their lives and their relationships.

Offering his guests a cup of coffee, Professor Johnson went into the kitchen and returned with a large pot of freshly brewed coffee plus an assortment of cookies. He also brought out a variety of cups. Some cups were porcelain, some were glass, some were crystal, some were very plain looking, others were very ornate, some were expensive, and somewhere exquisite. He invited each to select a cup and help themselves to the coffee. When all had selected a cup of coffee, the professor shared his thoughts. He began by saying:

"Notice that all of the nice cups were taken, leaving behind the cheap, plain cups. This might be considered typical. It is normal for you to want only the best for yourselves, but that is the source of your problems of stress and strife."

119

"The cup from which you are drinking adds nothing to the quality of the coffee. In most cases it is just more expensive. In other cases the cup hides what you drink. What each of you wanted was hot cup of coffee.

You didn't want the cup but you didn't consciously realize it, you went for the best cup. Soon you began to eye the other person's cup. And that merely added to your frustrations."

"Now consider this, **Life is the coffee**. Your job, your money, your position in society are the cups. They are the instruments to hold and contain life. The cup you have does not change the quality of the life you are living. Sometimes by focusing only on the cup we fail to enjoy the coffee . . . that God has provided for us."

"Always remember this, God provides the coffee and makes the finest brew. He does not choose the cup."

The happiest people don't have the best of everything. but they make the best of everything they have.

The motto is this:
Live simply.
Love generously
Care deeply
Speak kindly

Leave the rest to God. Remember the richest person is not the one who has the most, but the one who needs the least.

THE REAR VIEW MIRROR

Scripture:

"So do not fear, for I am with you
Do not be dismayed, for I am your God,
I will strengthen you and help you,
I will uphold you with my righteous right hand."
                                    Isaiah 41:10 NIV

The days of autumn had turned to winter and the strong winter storm had quickly move into the area. It was snowing heavily and blowing to the point that visibility was almost zero. Grace Mendoza had just gotten off work early and was making her way to her car in the parking lot. Good thing that she had remembered to put an ice-scraper and a snow brush inside the car. At least she wouldn't have to dig around in the trunk looking for something to remove the ice and snow from the windshield.

As she cleaned off the windows she wondered how she was going to make it home. Thanks to a good strong battery the engine started quickly and Grace got the heater and defrosters on and operating. She glanced at her fuel gauge and decided that there was an ample supply of gasoline to get her home. She sat in her car for a few minutes while it warmed up which gave her chance to review the situation.

Then she remembered the advice that her father had given her. If she ever got caught in a blizzard she should wait for a snow-plow to come along and follow it. That way she would not get stuck in a snow drift or run the risk of running off the road. Not a bad idea in conditions like this. It made her feel better and it wasn't long before a big truck with a snow plow came along. She started to follow the truck. She pulled in behind it and began to feel pretty snug about her decision. There didn't seem to be a problem even though the snow continued in blizzard conditions. Visibility was very poor but she kept the tail lights of the snow-plow in sight.

After about an hour had passed Grace was surprised when the snow-plow stopped and the driver got out of the truck. She watched as the driver inched his way back to her car and signaled her to roll down the window. The driver wanted to know if she was alright. He said that he could see her following him in his rear-view mirror. She thanked the driver and told him that she was fine. Then she began to tell him about her father's advice. "To follow a snow-plow if ever caught in a blizzard.

The driver smiled, brushed the snow off his cap and told her that it was okay with him if she wanted to continue to follow him. But he said, "I just finished plowing out **Wal-Mart** parking lot and I'm now headed over to **Sears** next."

Dear God help us to walk by faith and not by sight, trusting you every step of the way.

A cute story which could very possibly have happened. But there is a moral and a lesson to be learned from it. **Listen closely to God.** When trouble rages around us, like the snow storms of life often do, God has not moved away from us, we have likely moved away from Him. We need to return to him in faith and call for His strength. We often become comfortable and complacent in thinking that we can just "follow the snow-plow" when in truth what we need to do is learn to trust God and let Him lead the way.

In psalm 143: 8 David writes:

> *"Let the morning bring me word,*
> *Of your unfailing love.*
> *For I have put y trust in you.*
> *For to you I lift up my soul,*
> *Rescue me from my enemies,*
> *O Lord, for I hide myself in thee."*
>   *Ps. 143: 8 NIV*

•

HIDE IN THE CHERITH RAVINE

Two little boys, ages 8 and 10, were **excessively mischievous.** They were always getting into trouble. My wife's Father-in Law used to say: "**One boy, a whole boy . . . two boys, half-a-boy, . . . three boys, . . . no boy at all.**" And so it seems.

If any mischief occurred in their town, these two boys were probably involved. They were always getting into trouble and their parents knew about it. They just could not control the In desperation, the mother heard that a preacher in town had been successful in disciplining children, so she asked him if he would speak with her boys. The preacher agreed, but he said he would talk with them individually in his study. Please send them one at a time. The mother sent the 8 year old first, in the morning, with plans to send the 10 year old in the afternoon.

The preacher, a rather tall, husky man with a **booming voice**, sat the first boy down and sternly asked him, **"Do you know where God is, son?** The boy's mouth dropped open, but he made no response, sitting there wide-eyed not saying a word. The preacher repeated the question with even a sterner tone, **"Where is God?"** Again, the boy made no attempt to answer. The preacher raised his voice even more and shook his finger in the boy's face and bellowed, **"Where is God?"**

The boy screamed in terror, bolted from the room and ran as fast he could run, directly to his house and dove into the closet, slamming the door behind him. When his older brother found him in the closet, he said, **"What happened?** Why are you hiding in the closet?"

The younger brother, gasping for breath, replied, **"We are really in BIG trouble this time. GOD is missing, and they think we did it."**

Can you identify with this story? Maybe they needed to hide in the Cherith Ravine.

In the 17th **chapter of 1 Kings, verses 3-9,** we learn of the meaning of the **Cherith Ravine.** It was here that Elijah the prophet went into hiding, upon command of the Lord. Elijah had fought fiercely to preserve the true worship of God in his land, in spite of King Ahab and his wife Jezebel, who were turning the Israelite Kingdom into a nation of pagan believers and a cult of Baal. Baal was the most important Canaanite fertility god.

Elijah had warned King Ahab that the country would suffer a severe drought. To escape the King's wrath he went into hiding in a small isolated area east of the River Jordan that had a brook flowing through it. The location was known as the **Cherith Ravine.** While in hiding he drank from the brook and was fed bread and meat by the ravens. As promised, God supplied his basic needs.

God's servants must be taught the value of the hidden side of life. The person who serves in high positions, before others, must assume a lowly place before his God. We should not be surprised if God occasionally says to us, **"Dear child, you have had enough of this hurried pace, excitement and publicity. Now I want you to hide yourself—hide in the Cherith Ravine."** The Cherith Ravine may not be a location for us. Figuratively speaking, it might be sickness it might be sorrow, or a place of total solitude. A place away from the crowds that have turned our attention away from God.

Every soul that desires to wield great influence over others must first win the power in some Cherith Ravine experience. Acquiring spiritual power is impossible unless we absorb the power of the God through the gift of the Holy Spirit. May our lives be like the vegetation that lived centuries ago and absorbed the power of the sun and now gives back energy in the form of **coal.**

A DOG NAMED LUCKY

Mary and her husband Jim had a dog named Lucky. Lucky was a real character. Whenever Mary and Jim had guests for the weekend they would warn their friends not to leave their luggage open because Lucky liked to help himself to whatever he could reach. Inevitably, someone would forget and something would come up missing.

Lucky had a toy box in the basement and there was where all of treasures would be stashed; amid his other favorite toys. Lucky always put his finds in his toy box and he was very particular that his toys were in the box as well.

It happened that Mary found she had breast cancer. Something told her she was going to die of the disease . . . in fact she was sure it was fatal. She was scheduled for a double mastectomy. She was fraught with fear. The night before she was to go to the hospital she cuddled Lucky to her bosom. What would happen to Lucky? Although the three year old dog liked Jim he was very much Mary's dog. "If I die Lucky will be abandoned", she said. "He won't understand I didn't want to leave him." The thoughts made her sadder than thinking of her own death.

The surgery went well, but it was harder on Mary than her doctors had told her. Mary was hospitalized for over two weeks. Jim took Lucky for his evening walks but the little dog just drooped, whining and was generally miserable.

The day came for Mary to leave the hospital. When she arrived home she was so exhausted she couldn't even make it up the stairs to her bedroom. Jim made his wife comfortable on the couch and left her to nap. Lucky stood watching but he didn't come to her when she called. It made Mary feel even worse. She soon dozed off to sleep.

Mary woke up suddenly. For a moment, she couldn't understand what was wrong. She couldn't move her head and her body felt heavy and hot. Then she realized what had happened. She was covered, literally blanketed, with every treasure Lucky owned.

While she had been sleeping the sorrowing dog had made numerous trips to the basement bringing his beloved mistress all his favorite things. **He had covered her with his love.**

Mary forgot about dying. Instead, she and Lucky began living again, walking and playing together. It was been 12 years now and Mary is still cancer free. Lucky? He still steals treasurers and stashes them in his toy box, but Mary remains his greatest treasure.

Moral: *Live every day to the fullest. Each minute is a blessing from God. Never forget that people who make a difference in our lives are not the ones with the most credentials, the most money or the most awards. They are the ones who always care for us.*

In spite of illness, in spite of handicaps, even of sorrows, one can remain alive long past the usual date of disintegration if one is unafraid of change, is filled with faith, has an un-satiable intellectual curiosity, a interest in big things and is happy in small ways,

If you see someone without a smile today give them one of yours. **Live simply, Love seriously, Care deeply, Speak kindly, and leave the rest to God.** None of us want to get to the end of our lives and find that we have just lived the **length** of it. We want to have lived the **width** of it as well.

MEMORIAL DAY REFLECTIONS

Memorial Day will be celebrated on Monday May 27, this year. As a personal observation I believe that the country seems to be more aware of Memorial Day this year and will participate in it more passionately than in Memorial Days before.

Perhaps the War in Iraq and in Afghanistan has made us more cognizant. We are a peaceful Christian nation that finds itself embroiled in a war that seems to have no end, and yet, we know that it is essential that we fight for that which is right and what we believe is the will of God. "One nation under God, indivisible, with liberty and justice for all".

The price of gasoline has reached $4.00 or more a gallon, and seemly will go higher. We worry about the cost of electricity and heating oil and if we will be able to afford to heat our homes this winter. The housing market is depressed. Unemployment looms over the horizon for many workers. The cost of living continues to rise every time we go to the super market. It seems like we face a crisis every time we turn around. The Bible has some very good advice. Our resolve is found in the scriptures. Psalm 121:

> "I lift up my eyes to the hills, from where does my help come? My help comes from the Lord who made heaven and earth. He will not let your foot be moved. He who keeps you will not slumber. Behold he who keeps Israel will neither slumber nor sleep. The Lord is your keeper. The Lord is your shade on your right hand. The sun shall not strike you by day nor the moon by night. The Lord will keep you from all evil, He will keep your life. The Lord will keep you going out and coming in from this time forth and forevermore."
>
> Psalm 121

When we face the problems of this world and become anxious about our lives and the lives of our loved ones we need to read Matthew 6: 25-34:

> ". . . do not be anxious about your life, what you will eat or what you will drink nor about your body, what you will put on. Is not life more than food and body more than clothing? Look at the birds of the air, they neither sow or reap nor gather into barns and yet your heavenly Father feeds them. Are you not of more value than they? And which of you by being anxious can add a single hour to your life? Therefore, do not be anxious about tomorrow for tomorrow will be anxious for itself."
>
> Matthew 6: 25-34

We need to keep the solemn and sacred spirit of Memorial Day forever in our hearts and minds. We need to make it our traditional day of observance. This is the day that we honor our fallen heroes. Our fathers, our brothers, our sons and our daughters. It must be the day that we praise God and thank him for granting us freedom, and praise those who have sacrificed so much to preserve it.

One tradition that we have is the selling of poppy flowers by members of the Veterans of Foreign Wars. John McCrae wrote a classic poem as he looked out over the quiet battle fields known as **Flanders Fields** in World War I. He watched the wind blow the little red poppy flowers and wrote these words:

In Flanders Fields

In Flanders fields the poppies grow.
Between the crosses, row by row.
That mark the place; and in the sky,
The larks still bravely singing fly,

Scarce heard amid the guns below.
We are the dead. Short days ago,
We lived, felt dawn, saw sunsets glow.
Loved and were loved, and now we lie,
In Flanders fields.

Take up our quarrel with the foe:
To you from failing hands we throw,
The torch. Be yours to hold on high
If ye break faith with us who die,
We shall not sleep, though poppies grow,
In Flanders fields.

Traditionally we need to acknowledge and praise God for having allowed us the freedom that we enjoy.

"I will walk in freedom for I have sought out your precepts. I will
speak of your statutes before Kings and not be put to shame. For I
delight in your commands because I love them. I lift up my hands
to your commands, which I love and I meditate on your decrees."
Psalm 119: 45-48 NIV

Prayer

WALKING THE DOG

People seem to like dogs. Provided they are good natured, don't sleep on the couch, are house broke and don't chase cars. The writer Josh Billings said, "A dog is the only creature on earth that loves you more than he loves himself."

Perhaps you can reflect back to when you had a dog in your family. When my children were small we raised Collies and they were wonderful pets. Even when I would come home from work and the ground was wet and muddy our collie, Taffy, would greet me before I could get to the porch and put a nice big muddy paw print on my white shirt. The one I had planned to wear the next day.

All of the kids loved her. They all learned a favorite poem about Taffy: even to this day they will recite it:

> Taffy was a Welshman, Taffy was a thief.
> Taffy came to my house and stole a piece of beef.
>
> I went to Taffy's house, Taffy was not home.
> Taffy came to my house and stole a marrow bone.
>
> I went to Taffy's house, Taffy was in bed.
> I picked up the marrow bone and beat her on head.

I have often wondered why that little jingle was so popular. Perhaps it was because it had an element of violence in it, or simply it was about their dog.

Several years ago the house seemed a little empty so I talked my wife into getting a miniature dachshund. He only weighs 12 pounds but he has an ego the size of the kitchen. He would like to get out into the yard when the deer come around because he knows that he could take down a 185 pound buck. The only problem is when Fenway is bad, "Our dog" becomes "My Dog" and I end up in the dog house. John Hornbeck explains it this way: "A dog is an animal that teaches fidelity."

Having been in the aviation business I was amused by the following story:

A woman was flying from Melbourne, Australia to Brisbane on a commercial airliner. In route, the Captain came on the PA system and told the passengers that because of the weather at their destination they were required to divert to an alternate airport, Sydney. Upon their arrival there would very likely be a delay of about an hour. If any passenger wanted to get off the airplane the flight would **re-board in about 50 minutes.**

Everybody got off the airplane except for one lady who was blind. A man noticed her as he walked by her seat and knew she was blind because her guide dog lay quietly under the seat in front of her. He assumed that she had apparently flown this flight before because a crew member, the Captain, approached her, calling her by name. "Kathy," he said, "We are in Sydney and will be on the ground for over an hour. Would you like to get off and stretch your legs?" The blind lady replied, "No thank you, but maybe **Buddy** would like to stretch his legs."

All of the people in the gate area came to a complete stand still when the pilot walked off the airplane with a **guide dog.** The pilot was even wearing dark sun-glasses. The people scattered. They clambered trying to change planes, some even tried changing airlines. And so it is with appearances. So often we tend to jump at a conclusion or make a judgment based on what we think we see without getting all of the facts or knowing the whole story.

1 Samuel 16: 7 says, *"The Lord does not look at things man looks at. Man looks at the outward appearances, but the Lord looks at his heart."*

Remember things aren't always the way we think we see them.

May time be your friend.
May hope be your refuge.
May love be your guide.
May peace be your ally
May comfort be your keeper
And solace be your constant guardian

LOST GENERATION

I am a part of a Lost Generation, and refuse to believe that a dialog between us can change the world. This may come as a shock, but to believe **happiness** comes from within is a lie and that **money** will make us happy, is the truth.

In 30 years we will be telling our children **that they are not the most important things in our life.** What is mine is mine and does not belong to you." My employer will know that I have my priorities straight because, **"Work is more important than family."** I tell you this because once upon a time families stayed together, but this may not be true in our future generations.

We live in a quick-fix society. Experts tell us that in 30 years we will be celebrating the **10ᵗʰ anniversary** of our divorce. Statistics tend to support this hypothesis. It seems that we do not live in a country of our own making. In the future environmental decay and destruction will be the norm. No longer can it be said that we and our peers care about the earth. It will be evident that our generation is apathetic and lethargic. It is foolish to presume that there is any hope. And all of this will come true, unless, **we chose to reverse it.**

There is hope. It is foolish to assume that our generation is apathetic and lethargic. It will be evident that our peers and our children can be saved. It can no longer be said that environmental destruction is the norm. Marriage made with the love of God is accomplished with the promise of *"Till Death Do Us Part."*

In the future we will live in a country of our own making. We do not and cannot concede that in 30 years from now we will be celebrating the 10ᵗʰ anniversary of our divorce. I could tell you that this is a quick-fix society, but this is **not true.** Families will stay together with **welcome home signs,** and God's love, will prevail. **The Family** is much more important than work. I can tell you that this is not a quick-fix, I will have my priorities straight and I am a loyal employee, and my employer knows that my work is not the most important thing in my life.

So in 30 years my children will know and confirm that **"Money does not guarantee happiness. True happiness comes from within."** And they will agree it is false to believe that we are part of the **Lost Generation.** They will believe because they will know that there is a superior force who loves us. They will believe that we with God's help can overcome all adversity. We need to realize that there is a promise. Ephesians 6:10 tells us to **"Draw your strength from Him."** We must turn our attention away from the soothsayers and stop doubting ourselves. Don't be surprised when God calls you to step out in faith and do something that you don't feel qualified to do. That technique seems to be God's standard operating procedure. He does it so that we will lean more on Him, and less on ourselves.

Instead of being negative be positive. Does that mean we will never make a mistake or experience some failure? No! but instead of being discouraged look at it as part of a learning phase that will lead us on to greater things.

What kind of might is available to us? Boundless might! And where do we draw it from? The ultimate source—**GOD!** We are empowered and equipped as we work with Him. So, stop selling yourselves short. Armed with His spirit you will have more capability than you think you have. You will be able to do much more than you've ever done before. Cease being part of the **Lost Generation,** put your confidence in God.

Always remember to forget
The troubles that passed away,
But never forget to remember
The blessings that come each day.
Anonymous

COUNTING SHEEP

Sheep are said to be one of the most brainless animals in the world. They require constant attention and supervision. Sheep are generally kept in pens with other sheep called flocks and are attended by a person called a shepherd. When the shepherd goes to the pen to gather his sheep to take them to the pasture to graze, he calls to his sheep and they listen for his voice. He calls them by name and they recognize his voice as he leads them out of the pen. When the shepherd has lead all of his flock out of the gate the sheep follow obediently as he leads them away. The good shepherd knows each and every one of his sheep but sometimes the sheep will wander aimlessly if he doesn't watch them very carefully. The shepherd must watch the sheep constantly because they may get themselves into threatening situations. A sheep's life sounds rather hopeless.

Man is considered to have a much higher intelligence level than a sheep. Yet at certain times in our lives we also require constant maintenance and supervision. We hang out with the wrong groups and blend into crowds that lead us into threatening situations. If we go astray, we often go from task to task looking for the right thing to do, the right career to follow, the right spouse to choose, and so forth. In many ways we can be compared to the stupid sheep.

Humans have a lot to think about these days. We often think that we can do it ourselves without any help from anyone else. We often become oblivious to our Shepherd and our Savior who wants to help us.

When flocks mingle and graze together they become a large flock. but each sheep knows its shepherd and when he calls they recognize his voice. They immediately return to him. A shepherd is very guarded about his sheep. If one is missing or has gone astray he will go searching for it. He will call for the lamb and then listen carefully until he hears its cry. Once located the shepherd will recover the lamb and take it back to the flock. There is a bond between the shepherd and his sheep and it is never broken.

Jesus used parables to teach his followers. A parable can be described as an *"Earthly story with a Heavenly meaning."* In the agricultural society that existed at Jesus' time, Jesus spoke to his people in terms that were familiar to them so that they could understand what he wanted to teach them. In John 10:14 Jesus explains:

> "I am the good shepherd; I know my sheep and my sheep know me. Just as the Father knows me and I know the Father—and I lay down my life for the sheep. I have other sheep that are not of this sheep pen. I must bring them also. They too will listen to my voice and there will be one flock, and one shepherd. The reason my Father loves me is that I lay down my life—only to take it up again. No one takes it from me but I lay it down of my own accord; I have authority to lay it down and authority to take it up again. This command I received from my Father."
>
> John 10: 14-18 NIV

Jesus doesn't have to count his sheep. He is always right here with us. No matter where we wander or how far we go we must always learn how to cry out and then listen to hear his voice. We can let go of fear, and worry and be secure in the promise that Jesus, our Shepherd will save us. Amen

LIFE'S CHOICES

A young man went cross country skiing in the San Juan Mountains of Colorado with a group of friends. He became separated from the ski party, got lost, and spent three days in below-zero weather before he was found. Somehow he managed to survive. He spent several days in the hospital at Montrose for treatment of frostbite and exposure. But the frostbite condition had progressed to gangrene in his feet and the local surgeons wanted to amputate. The young man had some initial surgery done and for three weeks the outcome was very uncertain. Finally a decision was made to fly the patient to New York where it was hoped the world-renowned vascular team at John-Hopkins could avoid having to make the difficult choice of amputation.

The left foot began to improve, but the right foot became steadily worse. The time for amputation was at hand. The young man flatly refused. He preferred to keep his foot attached. Gradually he became sicker and sicker as the poison from his injured foot began to flood his body. His family and his friends were desperate. They tried to advise him but he just wouldn't listen.

Late one evening the situation came to a head. The attending doctors and staff reviewed the worsening condition with the patient. In the midst of the discussion. the man's fiancée, over-whelmed by the fact that her beloved would die; weeping tore off her engagement ring and thrust it onto the swollen black toe of his right foot. "I hate this damned foot," she sobbed. "If you want this foot so much why don't you marry it?" "You are going to have to choose, you can't have us both."

Everyone looked at the bright diamond, surrounded by the black and rotting tissues of the foot. Even under the fluorescent lights, it sparkled with life. The young man said nothing and closed his eyes with weariness. The next day they scheduled his surgery.

A year passed. After several months convalescing, the fitting of an artificial foot and a lot of physical therapy and rehabilitation, the young man was able to walk with only a slight limp.

The attending Doctor asked him, **"What changed your mind about the surgery?"** He said, "Seeing the diamond on my toe shocked me." Jenny, his fiancée was right. He had been attached to his foot and her dramatic gesture had helped him to see, for the first time, that he had to make a commitment to have it amputated. Ironically, it was his attachment to life that made him cling to it and drove him to persevere, enabling him to survive, alone in the snow, for three days, on that frigid mountain slope.

While **attachment** has its source in the person, in what the Buddhist's refer to as *"desire nature"*, it is **commitment** that comes from the soul.

The Bible says, *"God said, let us make man in our image and in our likeness."* Gen. 1:26 We are attached to God because we have been made in His likeness. But, God desires our **commitment.**

Modern life has made us people of attachment rather than people of commitment. Many find it difficult to tell the difference between attachment and commitment. Yet attachment leads us further and further into entrapment. Commitment, may sometimes feel constricting but will ultimately lead us to a greater degree of freedom and satisfaction.

Attachment is a reflex, an automatic response, which often may not produce our deepest blessing. Commitment is a conscious choice to align ourselves with our Lord and his genuine values and our sense of purpose.

> 2 Chronicles 16:9 says, *". . . the eyes of the Lord range throughout the earth to strengthen those whose hearts are fully committed." NIV*

Solomon's prayer of dedication and commitment reads:

> "O Lord, God of Israel, there is no God like you in heaven or earth.
> You who keep your covenant of love with your servants.
> Who continue wholeheartedly in your way.
> You have kept your promise to your servant David, my father,
> With your mouth you have promised and your hands fulfilled,
> As it is today."
>
> 2 Chronicles 6: 14-15. NIV

STOP AND TAKE A BREAK

Something to think about: *Yesterday is history*
Tomorrow is a mystery.
Today is a gift
That is why it's called
The present.

My wife Audrey loves to work in the flower gardens around our home. She has planted some interesting plants, **The Butterfly Bush, The Montauk Daisy, Snap Dragons, Oriental Daisies** and many more beautiful and colorful flowers. We like to see humming birds, and the butterflies that are attracted to the pollen in the flowers.

Along with the humming birds and the butterflies we see an endless string of **Honey Bees.** At first we were very cautious about disturbing these little creatures in fear of being stung. But after a while we found that if we didn't threaten them and let them go about their chores they would be oblivious to our presence.

> **The psalmist said to God** *"How sweet are your words to my taste, sweet than honey to my mouth."*
> **Psalm 119: 103**

But that is way with the honeybee. It is known for its ceaseless labor. Its hive is a hot-bed of activity. No wonder. A single worker bee makes $1/12^{th}$ of a teaspoon of honey in her lifetime. A good hive will produce **50** to **60** pounds of honey to survive the winter. The work never ends! And the numbers are almost beyond calculation.

Still, it's a little known fact that even the hard working honeybee will find a spot on the comb to cease all activity—and do absolutely nothing for a while. Nothing productive as far as the world is concerned. But this time of refreshment and renewal is absolutely essential. Bees seem to

138

require a little time away from the busyness of life. And it doesn't hurt the hive at all. Perhaps we can learn a lesson from the honeybee that will make our lives a little sweeter.

Many of us discover that our levels of stress and anxiety rise because of the never-ending tasks that fill our days. We worry about whether we can keep up. We try, but often fall short. Perhaps we can learn a lesson from the honeybee. We need to simply follow her example, just stop and take a break.

In today's business world we find that more and more corporations have a vacation and time off policy that requires their employees to take their vacations each year and not to accrue the time off. Like the honeybee it is found that the employee is more productive and better adjusted if he "takes a break."

Life is a busy endeavor. When we think of the little honey bee and the work it does to produce a teaspoon of honey in comparison to what God did to create the heavens and the earth we stand amazed. In our own lives there is always more things to do more places to go, and more people to meet than we can manage.

Stop and take a break from the busyness of life so that you can refresh your soul.

STOP AND TAKE A BREAK

A Poem

Life can make us weary and stressful most the time.

We need to stop and ask the Lord to help our spirits shine.

Take time to quietly bless our souls before we ever speak,

Reflect your never ending love for every one we seek.

We give our hopes and dreams to God, then leave them in

His hands. We know that with your Godly love you care for us,

To fulfill what you have planned.

If I can do some good today, or help in what I say,

If by my deeds Your love conveys a true and righteous way.

Dear Lord, just show me how.

Rev. Al Schmid

THE COURAGE CYCLE

I believe that we have cycles of being encouraged and discouraged. C. S. Lewis defines **courage** as, *"Not simply one of our virtues but the form of every virtue at the testing point, which means the point of highest reality."* The verb **encourage** means to give courage to or help. When you feel encouraged, you feel as though you could fly without wings. You are full of energy and take on tasks with zeal. You feel like you can accomplish the impossible.

But when you are discouraged you are listless. You feel zapped of your energy. Your boldness is drained away. Whatever power you had is gone and you feel worthless. Let's call it the **Courage Cycle.** At the peak of your courage cycle you are ready to take on the entire world. But for any number of reasons, even before the day is done you may hit the bottom of the cycle. You have become completely discouraged.

Experiencing discouragement is like feeling emotionally beat up. You feel as though your train has "jumped the track" and the rest of the world rushes on. You feel like a social failure, alone. There is the key component to discouragement; **"You feel alone."** Everyone goes through the cycle. Everyone from your children to your friends and co-workers and your associates. They too are going to feel discouraged and when they do they will feel alone. That makes it easier to know how to encourage someone. Often all it takes is to let them know that, **"You are not alone."** and someone cares.

It can be as simple as stopping by someone's house or office and cracking a joke or telling a story. A quick e-mail can do the trick. Send a greeting card or a little note. The shortest message can be powerful medicine because it attacks discouragement at the foundation by declaring, **"You are not alone."** Greeting someone you see by their first name simply says that you care about them, they are not alone and God loves them. The key to encouraging people—building them up, is to remind them of their strengths. Let them know that they matter and that they have an important place in the world.

What if you are discouraged? No one comes to visit you. No one helps you with encouragement. You don't get any phone calls or emails or cards. Here is a basic principle in life, **"Give and it will be given unto you."** So if you are discouraged don't wait for someone to come along and help you. Take the initiative and look around for someone else who is down and you reach out to them. Be there for them. Build them up. And a strange thing will happen. When you are there for someone else you suddenly are, **"Not alone."** Get the point? Encouraging someone else encourages you.

Interestingly, even if two discouraged people get together to have their own private "Pity Party" they end up encouraging one another because they realize that they are not alone. Perhaps that is why two people having lunch together is such an important event. Men don't know the importance of "A Girls Night Out" because it enables the ladies to share their concerns and let each other know that they are not alone.

In the process don't overlook the importance of including God in your life. He will listen to your problems, share your concerns and convince you that you are not alone. Webster defines alone as, **"With no other."** God is always with us and gives us endless love. We are never alone with Him. Amen.

Prayer

TEARS OF A WOMAN

A little boy asked his mother, "Why do you cry?" "Because I am a woman," she said. "I don't understand," the boy replied. His mother hugged him and said, "And you never will."

Later the little boy asked his father, "Why does mommy cry?" All women **cry for no reason,"** is all that his father could say.

When he became an adult the little boy asked God, Why do women cry so easily." God softly replied, When I created woman she needed to be special. I created her shoulders strong and broad enough to bear the weight of the world and yet soft enough to be comfortable."

God continued, "I gave her the strength **to give life**, and the strength that accepts the rejection that often comes from children. I gave her the strength to allow her to go on when everybody else gives up. I made her the kind of person who takes care of her family despite illness and fatigue. I gave her the sensitivity to love her children unconditionally, even when they have hurt her deeply. I gave her the strength to endure her husband's faults and inconsistencies and to stay at his side without weakening."

And finally, God said, "I gave her tears to shed whenever she needs to shed them." "You see my son," God continued, "The beauty of a woman is not in the clothes she wears, or the shape of her face, or the way she does her hair. Her beauty resides in her eyes. A woman's eyes are the doorway to her heart. The door to where **Love** is. The Love in your heart isn't put there to stay . . . because Love isn't Love until you give it away. And it is often through her tears that you can see her heart.

The world needs to know that all beings are beautiful, especially to those who have made you. Those who made you smile and laugh but occasionally shed a tear when you needed it the most. Those who made you see the good things, when you may only see the bad or the very worst."

God says that a tear is the way a woman expresses her **joy**, her **sorrow**, her **pain**, her **disappointments**, her **love**, her **loneliness**, her **grief** and her **pride**. Never discount a woman's tears.

We know that tears are not limited to women. Men shed tears as well. Even Jesus shed tears. In John 11:35, the shortest verse in the Bible, we read: "Jesus wept." "There are two ways to live your life. One is as though nothing is a miracle. The other is as though everything is a miracle." *Albert Einstein*

A beautiful story in Luke tells of how Jesus was anointed by a sinful woman. One of the Pharisees invited Jesus to his house to have dinner with him. As they were reclining at the table, a woman who had lived a sinful life, learned that Jesus was eating at the Pharisees' house and she came bringing an alabaster jar of perfume. She stood behind Jesus at his feet and started weeping and her tears began to wet his feet. Then she wiped his feet with her hair, kissing them and pouring perfume on them. The host was shocked to witness this behavior and challenged Jesus by asking, "What kind of woman is she? Don't you know that she is a sinner? How can you allow her to touch you?"

Jesus' reply was simple, he said, "I came to your house and you did not give me any water for my feet. But this woman wet my feet with her tears and wiped them with her hair. You did not give me a kiss but she has not stopped kissing my feet. You did not put oil on my head but she poured perfume on my feet. Therefore, I tell you, her many sins have been forgiven—for she **loved much.** But he who has forgiven little loves little." Luke 7:38 NIV

In Revelation we find this promise: John speaks of the New Jerusalem.

> "Now the dwelling of God is with men, and he will live with them. They will be his people, and God himself will be with them and be their God. He will wipe every tear from their eyes. There will be no more death or mourning or crying or pain, for the old order of things has passed away."
>
> Revelation 21: 3-4 NIV

God's promise is that he will make everything new.

WHAT ARE YOU WORTH

If someone were to approach you and ask, "What Are You Worth?" What would you say? It might create more questions than answers. You might ask, "Do you mean what is my **net worth?**" If I take inventory of all of my assets, add up their value and subtract the sum of my liabilities what would my banker or my accountant say I was worth?

Ask your best friend the question: "What do you think I am worth?" You might be surprised at the answer. It might be an entirely different opinion than what you expected. Depending on how close you are with your friend, it may be very interesting.

What about your children? What do you think they would say if they were asked that question? You might get a whole different idea of your relationship with them. Ask your boss or your supervisor the question, "What am I worth?" The answer would very likely relate to your job description and how well you performed. If you are in sales your worth might be reflected in the gross sales or revenues that you produce for the company. If you are an administrator the "worth" question would very likely depend on your professionalism, attitude and how well you did your job. How important are you to your company's profitability? A great deal I would trust. But certainly all of the answers are subjective.

Doctor, Lawyer, Indian Chief, politician, parent or paper boy each has their measure of worth. Ask your husband or wife, "What is my worth?" The answer might be very enlightening or even embarrassing. They might say, "You are worth the whole world to me," particularly when you mow the lawn, shovel the snow and take out the garbage, and by the way, I have been meaning to tell you, next time you take the trash out of the cellar don't forget the stack of papers next to the washer."

So we might conclude that our **Worth, or Value,** is directly related to and measured by the person or entity that knows us best. Perhaps at this time of year that might even include the IRS. But more importantly, we might ask what is our worth to God? The Bible says that we are made in the image of God. (Gen. 1:26) ***Then God said, "Let us make man in*** *our image in our likeness and let them rule over the fish of the sea and the birds of the air, over the livestock, over the earth and over all of the creatures that move on the ground." Gen. 1:26*

So when we look at our worth through Christ's eyes, we see that He values us even though we are sinners. Why else would the Savior have died for us? There is **no room** for human pride or self love, every bit of our worth comes from God.

God cares for us. He cares for **you**, He cares for **me**, and He cares for all of the people on earth.

> Luke 12; 6-7. *"Are not five sparrows sold for two pennies? Yet not one of them is forgotten by God. Indeed, the very hairs of your head are all numbered. Don't be afraid; you are worth more than many sparrows."*

> Paul wrote in Galatians 2: 20, *"I have been crucified with Christ and I no longer live, but Christ lives in me. The life I live in the body, I live by faith in the Son of God who loved me and gave Himself for me."*

His measureable sacrifice tells us that we are of great worth!

> His hands and feet and heart, all three,
> Were pierced for me on Calvary.
> And here and now, to Him I bring
> My hands, my feet, my heart. an offering.

The Death Of Christ' is the measure of God's Love for us . . . and thereby establishes Our Worth.

DON'T WAIT FOR THE PERFECT CONDITION

"HE WHO OBSERVES THE WIND WILL NOT SOW."
Ecclesiastes. 11:4 (NIV)

How often do we find ourselves standing on the dock waiting for the ship to be in place with the gangways perfectly positioned, the weather just right, the provisions stored aboard and an engraved invitation to go sailing before we are willing to launch out? It will never happen. Dreams do not move toward us, we have to move toward them.

It is time to stop waiting for perfection, inspiration, permission, reassurance, someone to change, the right person to come along, the new administration to take over, an absence of risk, a clear set of instructions, more confidence, or for the pain to go away.

Instead of saying I can't do that, or I don't have the resources, we need to know that "Necessity fuels invention." Instead of saying I have never tried that before we need to say let's give that a try. Instead of saying it will never get any better, we need to try it one more time. Instead of saying let someone else deal with it, we need to be ready to learn something new. Instead of saying, "It's not my job," say, "I'll be glad to take the responsibility." Instead of saying, "I can't," say, **"By God's grace I can."**

When I was a lad my father asked me to prepare the yard behind the house for a new lawn. It needed to be cultivated, raked and made ready for seeding. I worked at the task for several days thinking it would never be complete. Finally, it came time for planting. But it was a windy, stormy day and I didn't think it wise to continue with the job. I was reminded of the scripture: *"Whoever watches the wind will not plant; whoever looks at the clouds will not reap."* **Ecclesiastes 11:4.** When dad came home from work that night he was not happy with my decision not to plant the seeds.

He reminded me of the scripture: *"Sow your seed in the morning, and at evening let your hands be idle, for you do not know which will succeed, whether this or that, or whether both will do equally well."* **Ecclesiastes 11:6.**

For us to accomplish a task or to complete a project we cannot spend all of our time thinking about what must be done. Instead we need to reflect on what we have already accomplished and what we have learned from the results. Football coach John Wooden said, "**Things turn out best, for the people who make the best of the way things turn out.**"

There is a strong relationship between our movement toward our dreams and the resources we need becoming available to us. Too often we want to be able to see the resources or even have them in hand before we start moving forward. When we do this we have neither the resource or the movement.

We need to be like the snail that began climbing up an apple tree one cold wintery day. As he inched his way upward a worm stuck its head out of a crevice in the tree and said, "You are wasting your energy. There isn't a single apple on this tree." The snail kept on climbing and replied, "No, but there will be by the time I get there!"

Over and over in the Scriptures God sent his people out with what seemed to be little or no resources. But when they got to where God wanted them to be, the resources needed to get the job done were in place waiting for them. Vision does not follow resources, it happens the other way around. First we have a dream, then we have to move toward it, then the resources follow.

A wise man once said, "Effort only releases its reward after a person refuses to quit." People who succeed see what other people don't. That is what keeps them moving forward. It was by faith that Moses left the land of Egypt, not fearing the king's anger. He kept right on going because he kept his eyes on the one who is invisible.

CHURCH WHERE GOD'S PEOPLE GATHER

Ever so innocently, we have allowed our English language to distort the meaning of words. For example, the word **right**. Right, is an adjective that we use frequently. It can mean *correct or true*. It is the opposite of left, it means good or proper. It also infers justice. It implies what things ought to be, "the right of free speech, or to speak our mind." It is our claim to freedom of speech. Politically, it refers to a party with conservative views, and the action to set things in order or recover. And it can mean to recover in an upright position. "The ship was righted." We often use it in slang with the answer to a question. "**Right.**" or meaning that we understand.

Likewise, the word **church** has different meanings. Sometimes the word church means a place, as in (I left my Bible at the church.) Often it refers to an activity, as in (What times does church begin?) Often the word church is used to describe an institution, as in (This behavior is frowned upon by the church.) While these definitions are appropriate they miss the meaning of what church is all about.

The essence of church is the Christian family. Those people around the world who believe in and follow Jesus Christ. They commit themselves to Him and to each other. We tend to forget the meaning of ecumenical which means *"Belonging to the whole Christian Church."*

Baptists recognize believers of other denominations as "brother and sisters in Christ" and cooperate with them in those things which can be better accomplished together than separately. One definition of church is that it is not a club of saints or a private group but rather a hospital for sinners. Perhaps you remember this jingle:

This is God' house, but 'tis not to be deplored,
More people come to see the house,
Than serve the risen Lord.

The apostle Paul wrote about the church. He wasn't talking about a building, a place, an activity or an institution. For Paul, the word church meant a personal relationship among Christians. He often compared the church to the human body.

In the body all parts and details are important and they must function in harmony:

- If one member of the body is injured or sick or grieving or in trouble the entire body suffers.
- All members must operate in unison because if they try to go in different directions they can't go anywhere.
- Some members are more visible than others while some play a vital role on the inside. But all of the parts are necessary. There are no small parts in the body of Christ.
- If all of the members of the church were the same, the body would really look weird and it would not function well. Can you imagine a 5 foot, 8 inch long nose? You certainly would have an excellent sense of smell but you might look more like an elephant than a person. And it would be very difficult to drive a car.

The next time you are in church don't look at the building, or the contents. Stained glass windows are so alluring they might divert your attention. Instead look at the people. Appreciate them for who they are, what they need, and what they contribute to the body. Then look at yourself. What is your purpose? What is your role in the functions of the church and how do you fit in? Are you making a contribution to the over-all health and fitness of the body. Then ask yourself, "What more can I do to enhance the church?

Being part of the church means a lot more than just attending a service on Sunday morning and tossing a few coins in the offering plate, and shaking the Pastor's hand on the way out. Being a part of the church includes an inter-active relationship between people with Christ as a common bond.

With that kind of definition you can't be a **"Sunday Only Christian."** It means you must be a part of the body all week long. Don't leave your Christianity at the door when you leave this service, take it with you to savoir throughout the week.

Paul's letter to the Ephesians, Chapter 4: versus 17-24 says:

". . . You must no longer live as the Gentiles do, in the futility of their thinking. They are darkened in their understanding and separated from the life of God, Because of the ignorance that is in them due to the hardness of their hearts. Having lost all sensitivity they have given themselves over to continual lust for more. You, however, did not come to know Christ that way. Surely you heard of him and were taught in him in accordance with the truth that is in Jesus. You were taught, with regard to your former way of life, to put off your old self. Which is being corrupted by its deceitful desires; to be made new in the attitude of your minds. and to put on your new self, created to be like God, in true righteousness and holiness."

Ephesians 4: 17-24 NIV

TRUE FAITH

Several years ago I worked for Aero Commander Corporation, a division of Rockwell-Standard Corp,. located in Bethany, Oklahoma. The company manufactured airplanes. The Aero Commander line included an executive jet, a twin engine turbo prop and a series of piston driven light twins. It was a great job. I was able to fly all of the airplane models that were being built and my job was to conduct a Sales Training Program that taught the distributors how to sell the product.

The family, my wife and five children, moved from Illinois to take on this new challenge. We were all excited about being in a new community, joining a new church, enrolling in new schools and moving into a new home with five bedrooms and seven baths. The dream of a young rising executive.

We loved Oklahoma City. The kids made many friends. I kidded my youngest daughter about how she was developing an "Oakie" accent. Life was good. But then the "Dark Clouds" began to form. They weren't tornadoes, but we did see several of them during our stay in Bethany. Rockwell-Standard chose to merge with another large company, North American Aviation and became known as North American-Rockwell. Mergers always mean change. The companies change, the jobs change and the people change. Locations change.

The executive team of North American Rockwell decided to move all of the top management people from Aero Commander to Pittsburgh so that they could consolidate the staffs and keep everyone in one location. That meant that if I wanted to keep my job I had to relocate my family to Pittsburgh, Pennsylvania.

The moved required that we put our new home on the market. We had to make plans to move to Pennsylvania. The kids had to say goodbye to their friends at school and in the neighborhood. We had to leave out beloved church. We needed to find a new place to live in Allison Park, Pennsylvania, We did everything possible to make the move as simple and as easy as we could.

When the day came to move we were prepared, or at least we thought we were prepared. I had made a last minute decision to replace the old car with a new eight passenger station-wagon to make the trip to Pennsylvania more enjoyable. I took delivery of the new vehicle on the actual moving day and we loaded it up for the trip.

The trip was complex. We didn't want to wear the kids out so we planned to drive from Oklahoma City to Joplin, Missouri about 185 miles and stay overnight. Then the next day, Saturday, drive to Springfield, Illinois, our home town. Sunday, after church and dinner we would drive to Indianapolis, Indiana, overnight and continue to Pittsburgh on Monday. My secretary helped with the reservations because we needed three rooms at each motel stop. One for the girls, one for the boys, and one for Mom and Dad.

With the wagon loaded we were ready to go. Whoops! The kids were hungry. We hadn't had any supper. That is easy, we could stop at the local Burger-King and get something to eat. Here is where the problem started. My oldest daughter had to go back to the car and get something out of the rear seat. When she returned to the table she told us that she could not get the rear window to roll up. Upon checking I found the glass had slipped out of the channel and we had to work carefully to get it back in place. This complicated working the rear tailgate.

After the delay, we started again. The trip went well. The kids were asleep and quiet. Then it started to rain. Just a light drizzle. We had placed our luggage in the roof top carrier but I didn't have time to properly cover it. Oh well, not much can happen. Except that it began to rain harder and more steadily. Finally my wife insisted that I stop and check the luggage.

Yikes! Two suite cases containing the boys clothes had come loose from the tie-downs and had fallen off the rack. Lost! What do we do? We can't go back. We are on the Oklahoma Turnpike, a toll road, with limited access. We couldn't go back, or turn around. We had to continue to the next toll station. Which we did under great stress.

Often in life we are confronted with similar situations. We can't turn around or retrace our steps. We have no choice but to find the courage to go forward. It is then that we must have **True Faith** in God to take us safely through.

Albert F. Schmid

Our faith prevailed and in spite of our difficulties we completed our trip, nearly on schedule, but with a renewed faith and conviction.

Our scripture says: *"When thou passest through the waters, I will be with thee: and through the rivers, they shall not overflow thee."* Isaiah 43:2 (KJV)

Prayer: Dear Lord, help us to rest in the assurance that you will be with us when problems seem to overwhelm us. Amen.

PERCEPTION, TASTE AND PRIORITIES

Perception. Isn't that a neat word? Webster defines perception as: *"The intuitive recognition of the truth."* So I called this devotional: **Perception, Taste and Priorities.**

Scripture: Deuteronomy 29:2-9

> *Moses summoned all of the Israelites and said to them, "You have seen with your own eyes everything the Lord did in Egypt to Pharaoh and all of his servants and his whole country—all the great tests of strength, the miraculous signs, and the amazing wonders. But to this day the Lord has not given you minds that understand, nor eyes that see, nor ears that hear. For forty year I led you through the wilderness, yet your clothes and sandals did not wear out. You had no bread or wine or other strong drink, but He gave you food so you would know that he is the Lord your God." "When we came here King Sihon of Heshbon and King Og of Bashan came out to fight but we defeated them. We took their land and gave it to the half-tribe of Manasseh as their inheritance. Therefore, obey the terms of this covenant so that you will prosper in everything that you do."*
>
> Deuteronomy 29: 2-9 NIV

So, what is the lesson? Are we like the Israelites? Do we use our minds to understand? Do we see with our eyes the gifts that God has given us? Do we hear that which is good and praise God for it? Do we appreciate the gifts that the Lord has provided? Maybe we do and maybe we don't! Here is the story:

One cold winter day in January of 2007, a man played a violin in the Metro Station in Washington, D.C. He played six pieces from Bach.

It lasted for nearly an hour. During this time, about 2000 people went through the station, most of them on their way to work.

One man, of middle age, noticed the musician playing and slowed his pace, stopped for a few seconds and then hurried off to meet his schedule.

A few minutes later a woman walked by and threw a dollar in the hat and kept on walking. A short time later a young man leaned against the wall, listened for a while, looked at his watch and started to walk again. A 3-year old boy stopped, but his mother tugged on him and hurried him along. The boy stopped to look at the violinist again, but the mother pushed him hard and the child continued to walk turning his head, looking back. This scene was repeated again with several other children. Each parent, without exception, forced their youngsters to move on quickly.

The musician played continuously. Only six people stopped and listened for even a short time. About twenty people gave money, but continued to walk at their normal pace. The man collected a total of $32.75.

At the end of the hour the man finished playing and silence took over. No one noticed. No one applauded. There was no recognition and apparently little appreciation. No one recognized the violinist, **Joshua Bell**, one of the greatest musicians in the world. He played one of the most intricate pieces ever written by **Bach.** The violin he used was worth **$3.5 million dollars.** Just two days before, Joshua Bell played to a sold-out concert in Boston, where seats averaged more than $100 a piece.

This is a true story. Joshua Bell playing incognito in the Metro Station was organized by the **Washington Post** as part of a social-experiment about *Perception, Taste and People's Priorities.* The question was: **In an un-common place or environment, at an inappropriate time, do we perceive beauty? Do we stop to appreciate it? Do we recognize talent in an unexpected context?**

One possible conclusion reached from this experiment could be: If we do not have a moment to stop and listen to one of the best musicians in the world, playing some of the greatest music ever written, with one of the most beautiful instruments ever made. **How many other things are we missing?**

WHY DO WE PRAY

When I completed my term of service in the Navy, in the late '50s, I returned with my wife and two small children, to our roots in Springfield, Illinois. It was good to be back home after five years of service. We recognized the importance of finding a church home so we went back to South Side Christian, where we were charter members.

One Sunday at a fellowship dinner, which was held monthly, after the morning worship hour, one of the men of the church came to me and asked if I would lead the group in prayer. **I didn't know what to say.** I told him that my prayers had been limited to the times when the engines began to run rough or the thunderstorms were cracking outside the cockpit window, or the ice was forming on the wings. But, I asked the Lord to provide me with the words and I agreed to lead the members in prayer. And it worked! How many times have you faced a similar situation? Don't you wish that you had a way to offer a beautiful and eloquent prayer with little or no notice?

The average person thinks that praying means kneeling down and saying a few perfunctory, routine or superficial words. Prayer is more than that. It is one of the greatest skills in the world. It can be made beautifully simple and effective, but as with any skill, we must learn the formula and step by step open the circuit to receive the power. Prayer is talking with God. When we have a good friend we talk to that person about a lot of different things. That is part of being a good friend. In the same way we should talk to God about what is happening in our life. God wants us to share our life with him, to tell him about what makes us happy, what makes us sad, what frightens us. He wants to know what we want and what we would like him to do for us and for others we **know** and for whom we have concerns.

Consider these steps to develop your prayer life:

- *Talk to the Lord in simple, everyday language.* Talk to God about everything that is on your mind. and in your heart.
- *Tell God what you want.* Tell him that you want to have him provide you and if he thinks it would be good for you. Let God know that you will accept his decision as to what is best for you and for others.
- *Practice praying during the day.* Somehow we have gotten the idea that we should talk to God only a night, before we go to bed. We can talk with him at any time, even as we drive our car, or wait for the bus, or wait in a doctor's office, or where ever we are. If you have a friend you would talk with them. Then talk with God as you would with your friend.
- *Realize that words are not always necessary when you pray.* Just know that God loves you and he is always there to listen and to observe.
- *Try helping others with your prayers.* Pray not only for your family and your loved ones but also pray for people you do not like or have treated you badly. Chose someone who may be a problem to you and pray for them. Surround them with good will and faith. You will be amazed by the results.
- *Do not put all of your prayers in the form of asking.* Let your prayer consist of all the wonderful things that have happened to you. Name them one by one. Thank God for him hearing and answering your prayers.

Finally, consider this technique in praying:

The Five Finger Prayer

1. Your thumb, nearest you, reminds you to begin with those closest to you. They are the easiest to remember. Pray for family and loved ones. CS. Lewis describes it as, **"The sweetest duty."** Pray often.
2. Your pointing finger. Pray for those who teach, instruct, and heal. Include teachers, doctors, nurses, and ministers. They need God's support and wisdom and your prayers will be helpful.

3. Your middle finger. It is the tallest finger. It reminds us to remember the leaders of our nation; the President, the Senators and Representatives, the Governor the leaders in business and industry. May their decisions help to shape our country to preserve our freedoms and safe guard our future.

4. The fourth finger, is the weakest finger, ask any piano teacher. It should remind us to pray for those who are weak, in trouble or in pain.

5. Your smallest finger, often called the "pinky," is where we should place ourselves in relation to God and others. The Bible says, ***"The least shall be the greatest among you."*** The little finger should remind you to pray for yourself. After you have prayed for the other four groups your needs will be put into perspective and you will be able to pray for yourself more effectively.

The power of prayer is great and without limits. When we share our needs with God and thank him for the blessings we receive we will find peace. It is far more wonderful than the human mind can comprehend. God's peace will keep your thoughts positive and your heart pure. In Jesus precious name. **Amen.**

CHRISTIAN WITNESS

The word **Witness**, as defined in the dictionary is: "an attesting to a fact, statement, evidence, or testimony." A **Christian Witness** can be defined as one who testifies to religious beliefs of faith, as a Christian.

One activity that I engage in is going to the YMCA each day. I ride an exercise bike six miles. Part of my workout I spend watching the TODAY Show on TV and socializing with a group of friends. Each day Al Irby, the YMCA Trainer, comes by and asks," What is the Word of The Day?" We have been playing this game using an interesting or different word each day for some time. Yesterday the word was **"discombobulate, to** upset the composure of.' I asked Al if he knew the meaning—he hesitated and said, "To screw up."

One way of witnessing is through Christian communications. The art of Christian communication covers many aspects of the relationship between one Christian and another Christian and the whole world. The New Testament contains a number of helpful suggestions relative to how we can establish good communications. They are called the **"One Another Commands.**

These commands when followed, are a source of correct Christian communication. The commands could be looked at as God's code of conduct for Christian relationships. However, we do not naturally do the things that are commanded in the **"One Another's."** Christian communications is a skill we must choose to learn by submitting to the Word of God and by applying it to our lives.

Monday's word at the YMCA was **"fastidious**—very careful of matters of choice or taste." And so it should be. We can be fastidious about witnessing. The following is a list of some of the **"One Another"** commands found in the New Testament and related to Christian communications:

Love one another—John 13:34
Forgive one another—Ephesians 4:32

Be servants to one another—Galatians 5:13
Show hospitality to one another—1 Peter 4:7
Pray for one another—James 5:16
Do not speak evil of one another—James 5:9
Do not judge one another—Romans 14:13
Teach one another—Colossians 3:16
Have the same care for one another—1 Corinthians 12: 25-26
Be patient with one another—Hebrews 10:36
Love one another—John 13:34

And there are many more that will bear witness to our Christian faith. Each command in the list begins and ends with John 13:34 **"Love one another."**

I am reminded of the little girl who was in the Special Olympics. She came in last in every event she entered and had numerous blue ribbons. The colors of the ribbons awarded in the Special Olympics were opposite of the colors used in other events. Blue was given to those who finished. She didn't care about coming in last, but she wanted a different colored ribbon. Her grandmother told her that she was praying that God would send an angel to help her. The little girl was in her last event and running in last place when the girl in front of her looked back and then stopped to wait for her. Then they grasped hands and finished the race together. Both received white ribbons! Here is an example of Christian witness and an answer to prayer.

I believe that the Lord gives each of us an opportunity to witness. A friend of mine once said, "I knew that I should have said something to that person, but I didn't." My wife, Audrey, is always witnessing, and often thinks that she just doesn't make a difference, but she does. Last week she was in the checkout line at the local super market and she was standing in front of a young black, Army Officer who was in uniform. She turned to him and said, "My husband and I sincerely appreciate the fine job that you and your fellow National Guard members are doing. Thank you!" She told me that the young officer was so overcome that he almost started to cry. Sometimes it is just a smile, a friendly nod, a simple praise or even a "Word of the Day" that will make a blessing for the recipient and the giver. Be a Christian Witness.

Albert F. Schmid

"Do not conform any longer to the pattern of this world, but be transformed by the renewing of your mind. Then you will be able to test and approve what God's will is—His good, pleasing and perfect will."

Romans 12:2

Lord help me to look beyond myself, to reach out to others, and to draw them to you, in Jesus name. Amen.

PRACTICE YOUR FAITH

Pete McGraw was a friend and roommate of mine at Western Illinois State College in the late forties. We roomed together for the entire four years at school. We had a number of memorable experiences. Pete was a physical education major with plans to become a football coach at the high school level. I majored in business with a P.E. minor, so Pete and I shared many of the same classes. One of the things that we taught was the importance of each of the players on the football team to know the basics. They needed to understand the four basic principles of football. How to run, block, kick and throw. Our students may have understood the premise of the game but in order to become a winning team they needed to put them into practice and execute the plays together. Starting early in the fall we were involved in drill after drill in order to sharpen and co-ordinate their skills.

Our players, who were students at the college's training school, understood the principles but struggled to put them into practice. It often frustrated us since we wanted to produce a winning team. A couple of seasons were moderately successful, but otherwise we were ranked in the bottom of the league.

After graduation in 1951 Pete and I went our separate ways. Pete had served for four years in the United States Army. He attended school on the G.I. Bill. I went to college right after graduation from high school and during my college years had a draft deferment. My draft board gave me the option of enlisting in my choice of military service or they would draft me in 30 days. My decision was not difficult. I joined the U.S. Navy.

Pete got a position as a football coach at a small high school in northern Illinois. He apparently had learned his lesson well because he went on to become a very successful coach and ultimately the athletic director at a small college in Michigan. I served for six years in the Navy, became a Naval Aviator and in 1958 moved my family back to Illinois. Both Pete's career and mine were quite diverse but the moral principle was the same.

The Bible tells us how God wants us to live. He has clearly outlined the basics by which He expects us to live. Pete and I had done the same thing with the players at the training school at Western. Like the football players, we attempt to fulfill the will of God but often struggle to face the challenges and ordeals that we encounter. The football players practiced to become winners. We must practice our faith, and the more that we do, the stronger our faith becomes. We need to practice it every day. We show our faith as we obey and fulfill God's mandates in our lives. Often we find that it isn't very easy. God uses challenges that come when we are most vulnerable and least expect it in order to turn our weaknesses into strengths.

Like the football players on the winning team, when they applied the basic principles they eventually won the championship. Likewise, when we practice our faith we obtain spiritual victory. When we gain the prize of victory in Christ, our hearts will overflow with joy and blessing.

Scripture: *"Train yourself in godliness, for while physical training is of some value, godliness is valuable in every way, holding promise for both the present life and the life to come."*

1 Timothy 4: 7-8 (NRSV)

Keep practicing your faith until you get it right.

ULTIMATE FORGIVENESS

It was Monday morning. The men at the church had finished their prayer breakfast and Tom Dace had departed to go to a house that he was remodeling on Scarritt Street. He and a fellow worker were renovating a two story house in that area.

It wasn't long until the minister received a telephone call from Tom's wife asking him to hurry to the emergency room at the nearby hospital. When the Pastor arrived he went directly to the emergency room to find Tom in a critical condition. He had been assaulted by a man wielding a claw-hammer and the outlook was grim.

Tom was an Elder at his church. He taught the adult Bible Study Class. He was in his 70s and worked as an independent carpenter helping Christians find better homes in which to live. His wife Florence was also a Christian. She sang in the choir, taught Vacation Bible School, gave devotions, and was a steady worker in the church. She knew what she believed and would speak up for what she felt was right.

Frank Sherry was the assailant that fatal morning. He had taken a claw-hammer in a drunken, drug induced rage and attacked the two men who were remodeling the downstairs of the house in which he lived. He had mixed drugs and alcohol the night before and when the power saws and hammers used by the workmen started he said, "I thought they were aliens attacking." After striking Tom numerous times and Tom's fellow worker, he rushed out of the house and assaulted several other people. He was finally apprehended and subdued at the local drug store on the corner of South Grand and Sixth Street.

The attack was a horrible thing. It brought Christians from all over the area to the Chapel at St. John's Hospital that evening to pray for Tom and Florence and their family. The prayers continued night after night. Tom did not recover. When someone dies there are always tears of sadness, but there are also tears of joy. Sadness because we lose people we love, joy because of the eternal hope we have in Christ.

Something amazing happened! After Frank Sherry sobered up, Florence Dace went down to the jail to see him. She took Tom's Bible with her. After careful screening she was allowed to see Sherry. She said, "You have done a terrible thing . . . but my God says that if I want God to forgive me I must forgive others." "Frank Sherry I forgive you." One other thing that she told him, "You owe it to me since you killed my husband. **Take this Bible and read it, especially the part that is written on the inner cover. My husband has written how to become a Christian.**" The whole community learned of her courageous witness and were amazed that this woman could forgive the killer of her beloved husband. It demonstrated the ultimate act of forgiveness.

Sometime later, Frank Sherry called from the prison in Southern Illinois where he was incarcerated. He asked if Florence and her minister would come visit him. They accepted the invitation and when they arrived and proceeded through the security checks, they found Frank sitting at a table in the visitors area with his Bible in front of him. When he saw Florence he announced, **"I've been saved, I've been save."**

They came together and embraced one another, and all three wept. Frank kept asking Florence, "Do you really forgive me?" Every time they met after that he asked her the same question, "Do you really forgive me?"

Frank opened his Bible and read Jeremiah 17: 9, **"The heart is deceitful above all things, and desperately wicked: who can know it?"** Then he shared his life's story: He told of his young misspent life. The drug use, the alcohol, the degrading music and all. He wanted to escape this life so he joined the Navy. It wasn't long before he was addicted to the drugs, found out and given a dishonorable discharge. Now he was confessing his sins! Genuine forgiveness is preceded by a penitent heart. It was time for rejoicing.

15 year passed and Frank was paroled from prison. Florence had written to the Pardon Board year after year requesting his release. He was finally allowed to return home. He went to Florence's church and retold his story. Frank and Florence embraced and she said, **"My God tells me, 'If I want Him to forgive me, I must forgive others'."** "Amen."

Florence Dace became known as "The Woman who had Forgiveness in Her Eyes."

> Scripture: "For if you forgive men when they sin against you, your heavenly Father will also forgive you. But if you do not forgive men their sins, your Father will not forgive your sins."
>
> Matthew 6: 14-15

Prayer

GOING TO HEAVEN

There is a story about a minister who died and was standing in the line at the Pearly Gates waiting to enter the kingdom of heaven. Ahead of him was a fellow dressed in a loud shirt, leather jacket, jeans, wearing brown loafers with no socks, A real cool guy. Saint Peter addressed the cool guy. "Who are you?" he said, "I need to know whether to admit you to the kingdom of heaven." The fellow answered, "I'm Peter Pilot, retired Delta Airlines Captain from Los Angles." Saint Peter checked his list, smiled and said to the pilot, "Take this silken robe and golden staff and enter into the kingdom." The pilot goes through the Pearly Gates into Heaven.

Next it is the minister's turn. He stands erect and booms out, I am Joseph Snow, Pastor of Saint Ann's in Pasadena for the last 43 years. Saint Peter consults his list. He says to the minister, "Take this cotton robe and wooden staff and enter into the kingdom. "Just a minute," says the minister, "That man who said he was a pilot got a silken robe and golden staff and I get a cotton robe and wooden staff, how can this be?" "Up here in Heaven we work by results," answered Saint Peter, "While you preached people slept, while he flew people prayed."

A lot of people approach going to church in about the same manner. My wife and I have talked about what we want from church but never completely agree. No single church has everything that we agree is necessary for spiritual growth. But, most Sundays we have found something about the church to carry us through times of disillusionment and doubt. Here's what I have learned:

1. **Faith** is not me and God **alone.** Being with a group of believers is what matters. They can be irritating, exasperating and occasionally cruel, but they teach me that to love others means loving and forgiving those who can be unlovable.
2. Though **Sermons** don't always inspire, they do connect us to the word and gives us a view that rises above the clamor in which

we are drowning. On a good Sunday a sermon re-adjusts my perspective and renews my hope.

3. **Hymns** allow me to give expression to buried emotions. The tunes direct praise to the One who is the author of all that is. Without much outward expressions I can easily become obsessed with myself.

4. **Prayers** remind me that life isn't only about me. A community of faith is made up of individuals with joys, pains and desires that are unknown to others unless expressed petitions to God become opportunities for service and celebration.

5. I stay connected to church because it connects me with the One who loves me, and compels me to do the same for others. We go to church to worship our Lord and to be spiritually fed. We serve the Lord by working together to do His will. I know churches aren't perfect. Never have been and never will be. They get wrapped up in mundane matters, often overlook those who are hurting and fail to reach out to the most needy. And it can be, and often is, very frustrating. Sometimes it takes the eyes and ears of faith to recognize the presence of God in a church.

> *"If I have the gift of prophecy and can fathom all mysteries, and all knowledge and if I have a faith that can move mountains, but have not love, I am nothing. If I give all I possess to the poor and surrender my body to the flames, but have not love, I gain nothing."*
> *1 Corinthians 13:2 NIV*

We can do all types of philosophizing, but the bottom line is what we do to represent God in the way that we live our lives. Sometimes it is the simple, practical ways that are the most meaningful and have the best results.

Going to Church, do it with enthusiasm, love of God and love for your fellow man.

PRESCRIPTION FOR THE SOUL

This is a true story of a young man named Jack Jones who was an aggressive executive and had achieved apparent success in his life. He was well educated and had a very responsible executive position with a Fortune 500 company. He drove a new Lexus automobile and lived in a very pretentious suburban home. He was married to Ann a charming, attractive lady and they had three beautiful children, two boys and a girl. The wife drove a new Toyota SUV and belonged to several ritzy social clubs in town. They enjoyed their membership at a private country club and would often have dinner and cocktails there a couple times a week. On the surface it seemed that they were happy and content. Life was good!

But, unfortunately, Jack was very unhappy. He was stressed out. He couldn't relate to his children. He and his wife were contemplating a divorce. He couldn't get along with his fellow executives at work and his list of golfing buddies, who played golf with him every Sunday morning, had dropped to zero. Everything that he did seemed to go wrong. Life seemingly wasn't worth living. Jack could not decide what was the matter.

The answer may have been that Jack was looking **out** instead of **in**. That is to say that Jack was concentrating on the materialistic side of life rather that the spiritual side. He thought that money could buy happiness. His focus was centered on the affluent, rich life style that he thought he could create and to which he felt entitled.

Why wasn't Jack's life the success that he wished for? One of the problems with our society is we don't have time for God. It causes a lot of problems in our world today. We try to keep God in church on Sunday morning, sometimes on Sunday night and occasionally at a mid-week service but we don't have time or room for Him during our work or play. Because, like Jack, we think that we can handle it by our self.

When we are sick and we finally admit it, we usually go to the doctor to be examined and seek his medical advice. Often the doctor will give us a prescription with directions as to when and how much we should take. If we follow his directions we will likely feel much better soon.

And so it is with the prescription for the soul. We must admit that we need to do something about our spiritual health. Turn to the scriptures and find the prescription that you need. For example: The Apostle Peter writes in his epistle:

". . . prepare your minds for action; be self-controlled; set your hope fully on the grace to be given to you when Jesus Christ is revealed. As obedient children, do not conform to the evil desires you had when you lived in ignorance. But just as he who created you holy, be holy in all things that you do; it is written; be holy because I am holy."

I Peter 1: 13-16 NIV

PRESCRIPTION FOR THE SOUL

A Poem

I knelt to pray but not for long, I had too much to do.
I had to hurry off to work for the bills would soon be due.
I knelt and said a hurried prayer and jumped up from my knees,
My Christian duty now was done, my soul could rest at ease.
All day long I had no time to spread a word of cheer.
No time to speak of Christ to friends. They'd only laugh I feared.
No time, no time, too much to do. That was my constant cry.
No time to give to those in need. Even if I tried.
No time to spend time with my kids, to learn what they hold dear.
No time to teach them about the Lord, if only they would hear.
No time to share my life with Aud, the one I truly love.
I didn't think she needed help from Jesus Christ above.
Then the day of reckoning came. Not even time to cry.
No time to make a simple change. For it was time to die.
I went before the Lord and stood with down cast eyes.
For in his hand God held a book; it was the Book of Life.
God looked into his book and said, "Your name I cannot find.
I once was going to write it down . . . but never found the time."

Do we have time for God?
I certainly hope so, He has time for us.

BE QUIET AND LISTEN

"The words of the wise heard in quietness . . . are better than the shouting of a ruler among fools." Ecclesiastes 9: 17 (NASB)

Solomon, the writer of Ecclesiastes, was a wise and affective leader. He gained much wisdom and knowledge through his lifetime. God gave Solomon wisdom, but Solomon gained knowledge by observing and by developing his own attitudes toward life. It is well known, if only by common sense, that you cannot listen if you are talking. So, I dare say that Solomon was a good listener.

I am reminded of the cardinal rule that was observed at the dinner table in the ward room by the Navy pilots and officers as we ate our meals aboard ship or at the Naval Station. Three subjects that were forbidden and were never discussed were: Religion, Politics, and Sex. Someone once asked, "Well what else is there to talk about?" Perhaps we need to better understand the wisdom and attitudes of Solomon.

The passage in Ecclesiastes 9:17 bears witness to the fact that it is important to listen. It occurs to me that we have been engaged in an election year that seemingly has come to an end. The election is over but now we are asking the questions what is next. We have listened to the "shouting of candidates" and the various promises and declarations made by each until it is now time to "listen in quietness." As we regroup to begin the most important period in our history when it is critical to make the right decisions to sustain our country, its fate and our future, our freedoms and our well-being all which has been received from our God. We need to carefully and prayerfully consider our choices and act accordingly.

In order for the wise person to be heard there must first be silence of the listeners. This is in sharp contrast to those who have shouted in order to be heard above the drone of the foolish. Those who would rather argue than listen to the wisdom of the Lord are in great number. Be cautious about this.

God gave us the ability to speak, the ability to reason and the ability to make good decisions. We also have another important gift and that is the ability to listen. We can learn how to live a righteous life and how to truly help one another if we chose to listen. This perhaps is our most precious gift. While it is true that we must speak to ask questions, there is a point that we must close our mouths and open our ears in order to comprehend the answers. We have exercised our right to vote and to be heard. We have chosen our new leaders, we must now remain committed to doing the job to our benefit and the Lord's satisfaction.

1. We must support pro-life legislation, because God hates the shedding of innocent blood. (Prov. 6:17)
2. We must continue to support our allies in Israel because God blesses those who bless Israel and curses those who don't. (Gen. 12: 3)
3. We must ask our government to work on debt reduction, because the Bible tells us that "The borrower is the servant to the lender." Prov. 22:
4. We must lower our unemployment rate because God says, "If a man does not work, let him not eat." (2 Thess. 3: 10)
5. We all must agree that our government's purpose is to reward the good and punish the evil. (Romans 13)
6. We must insist that our elected officials adhere as closely as possible to complying with God's word. (2 Timothy 3: 16)
7. And we should know that whoever was elected, God was the one who put them in that authority. (Dan 12:21)

I urge you to speak quietly but succinctly. But at the same time think of the challenges we have as citizens of the United States of American and as children of God.

Amen.

COUNTING MY BLESSINGS PRAYER

Dear God: I know you're watching over me,
I'm feeling truly blessed
For no matter what I pray for,
You always know what's best!

I have this circle of special friends,
Who mean a lot to me,
Some days I send them messages
At other times, I let them be.

I am so blessed to have these friends,
With whom I've grown so close,
So this little poem I dedicate to them,
Because to me they are the "most."

When I see each name downloaded,
And view the message they've sent,
I know they've thought of me that day
And "well wishes" were their intent.

So to you my friend, I would like to say
Thank you for being part
Of all my daily contacts,
This comes right from my heart.

God bless you all is my prayer today,
I'm honored to call you my friend,
I pray that God will keep you safe,
Until we meet again.
                    Amen
                    Anonymous 5/11

THE COURAGE CYCLE

I believe that we have cycles of being encouraged and discouraged. C. S. Lewis defines **courage** as, *"Not simply one of our virtues but the form of every virtue at the testing point, which means the point of highest reality."* The verb **encourage** means to give courage to or help. When you feel encouraged, you feel as though you could fly without wings. You are full of energy and take on tasks with zeal. You feel like you can accomplish the impossible.

But when you are discouraged you are listless. You feel zapped of your energy. Your boldness is drained away. Whatever power you had is gone and you feel worthless.

Let's call it the **Courage Cycle.** At the peak of your courage cycle you are ready to take on the entire world. But for any number of reasons, even before the day is done you may hit the bottom of the cycle. You have become completely discouraged.

Experiencing discouragement is like feeling emotionally beat up. You feel as though your train has "jumped the track" and the rest of the world rushes on. You feel like a social failure, alone. There is the key component to discouragement; **"You feel alone."**

Everyone goes through the cycle. Everyone from your children to your friends and co-workers and your associates. They too are going to feel discouraged and when they do they will feel alone. That makes it easier to know how to encourage someone. Often all it takes is to let them know that, **"You are not alone."** and someone cares.

It can be as simple as stopping by someone's house or office and cracking a joke or telling a story. A quick e-mail can do the trick. Send a greeting card or a little note. The shortest message can be powerful medicine because it attacks discouragement at the foundation by declaring, **"You are not alone."** Greeting someone you see by their first name simply says that you care about them, they are not alone and God loves them. The key to encouraging people—building them up, is to remind them of their strengths. Let them know that they matter and that they have an important place in the world.

What if you are discouraged? No one comes to visit you. No one helps you with encouragement. You don't get any phone calls or emails or cards. Here is a basic principle in life, **"Give and it will be given unto you."** So if you are discouraged don't wait for someone to come along and help you. Take the initiative and look around for someone else who is down and you reach out to them. Be there for them. Build them up. And a strange thing will happen. When you are there for someone else you suddenly are, **"Not alone."** Get the point? Encouraging someone else encourages you.

Interestingly, even if two discouraged people get together to have their own private "Pity Party" they end up encouraging one another because they realize that they are not alone. Perhaps that is why two people having lunch together is such an important event. Men don't know the importance of "A Girls Night Out" because it enables the ladies to share their concerns and let each other know that they are not alone.

In the process don't overlook the importance of including God in your life. He will listen to your problems, share your concerns and convince you that you are not alone. Webster defines alone as, **"With no other."** God is always with us and gives us endless love. We are never alone with Him. Amen.

AERIAL TACTICS WITH A WINGMAN

A farmer was planting corn in his field in Wisconsin one morning when he looked up to witness an interesting aerial battle between a golden eagle and three crows. The eagle was being chased by three crows who were continually dive-bombing and pecking at its tail and wing feathers. Apparently the crows were retaliating because the eagle had tried to rob their nest.

The eagle was a large bird with a wing span of about six feet. The crows were relatively small in comparison. The eagle tried to get away from the crows but the attackers were vicious They continued their attack with a vengeance. The eagle banked hard to the right then to the left in an evasive maneuver and then as a defensive move, landed in the field not more than 100 feet from the tractor. The bird was a magnificent specimen standing nearly three feet tall.

The crows landed as well. They immediately took up positions around the eagle, but kept their distance at about twenty feet from the bird. The eagle would take a couple of steps to-wards one of the crows and the crow would hop backwards or forwards to keep a safe distance.

Then the eagle's wingman showed up. Eagles mate for life and are dedicated to their partner. The second eagle was there to help. It came hurtling down from out of the sky at top speed and just before it got to the ground the first eagle took off. (Obviously a coordinated tactic, probably pre-briefed.) The three crows who were watching the first eagle also took off thinking they were going to give that big bird more harassment.

The first crow being targeted by the diving eagle never had a chance. There was a mid-air explosion of black feathers and the crow was done. The diving eagle then banked hard left in what had to be a 9g climbing turn, using the energy it had accumulated in the dive hit crow #2 in less than 10 seconds. Another dead crow.

The grounded eagle, which was now airborne gained an altitude advantage on the third crow made a shallow dive, banked hard right and went after the crow who was streaking west in full after-burner. The escaping crow tried to evade the hit but it didn't work. Crow #3 bit the dust about twenty feet above the ground.

As the farmer worked his way across the field on his tractor he passed within twenty feet of one of the eagles who was finishing eating its catch. The eagle stopped eating and looked at the man on the tractor and gave him a look that convinced the farmer that the eagle knew that it was the "***Boss of the Sky.***" and should not be reckoned with.

The moral of the story is we might agree that the Eagle was the "Boss of the Sky," but the truth of the matter is, the Lord is the master of the sky, the earth, and the seas.

Psalm 147: 5-6 makes this abundantly clear.

> "***Great is our Lord and mighty in power,***
> ***His understanding has no limit.***
> ***The Lord sustains the humble***
> ***But casts the wicked to the ground.***"
> ***Psalm 147: 5-6 NIV***

A poem by Sir William Osler may re-focus our attention on the Aerial Tactics story:

> Lift up one hand to heaven and thank your stars if they have given you the proper sense to enable you to appreciate the inconceivably droll situations in which we catch our fellow creatures.
>
> Sir William Osler

Prayer

THE GOSPEL MESSAGE
SIMPLY STATED

The Good News refers to the teaching of Jesus Christ and the Apostles. The New Testament books, Matthew, Mark, Luke and John are called the Gospels. Each contains many stories and examples from which we can learn how to live a righteous, meaningful and happy life. However, there are other sources that are available in order to learn these essential lessons. The following story is a wonderful lesson, for all of us.

The story: Carl was a quiet man. He didn't talk much and stayed pretty much to himself. But he would always greet you with a smile and a firm handshake. Carl lived in the same neighborhood for more than 50 years but no one could really say that they knew him.

Before his retirement he took the bus to work each morning. The sight of him walking down the street often worried the neighbors. He had a slight limp from a wound that he had received in WWII. The neighbors feared that although he had survived the War he may not be safe in the changing downtown environment. The area had become infested with acts of crime, random violence, gang activity and drug dealing. It was happening in every large city in the country.

When Carl saw an announcement in the Sunday Church Bulletin asking for volunteers to help care for the gardens around the Church, he responded without hesitation. In his characteristically quiet, but unassuming way, Carl took the job. No fanfare, he just signed up.

Carl was eighty-seven years of age. It wasn't long before the very thing that his friends feared happened. He was watering the garden one day when three punk-gang members approached him. Ignoring their attempts to intimidate him Carl simply asked, "Would you like a drink of water from the hose?" The tallest and toughest looking of the three said, "Yeah old man, I'll have a drink." Carl offered the hose to him but the other two grabbed his arm throwing him to the ground. As the hose snaked crazily over the ground it doused everything in its way. Carl's assailants grabbed him and stole his retirement watch and his wallet, and away they ran.

Carl tried to get up but he had been thrown down on his bad leg. He lay there trying to help himself as the minister came running to help. "Carl are you okay?" asked the minister. "Are you hurt?" he kept asking as he helped him to his feet. Carl passed a hand over his brow and sighed, shaking his head. "Just some punk kids. I hope they will wise up someday."

His wet clothes clung to his slight frame as he bent down to pick up the hose. He re-adjusted the nozzle and began to water. Confused and a little concerned the minister asked, "Carl, what are you doing?" "I've got to finish my watering," was the reply, "It's been very dry lately." Satisfied that Carl was all right the minister could only marvel at what had happened. He believed that Carl was fine. He was a man from a different time and different place.

A few weeks went by and the three punks returned. As was the case the first time, they began to intimidate Carl. Carl did not over react. He again offered them a drink from the hose. This time they didn't rob him but they wrench the hose from his hands and drenched him from head to foot with icy water. When they had finished their assault they sauntered off down the street laughing and yelling catcalls and profanity. Carl just watched them go. Then he turned towards the warm sunshine, picked up his hose and went back to work.

The summer was quickly fading into fall. Carl was doing some tilling around the shrubs when he was startled by someone coming up from behind. He stumbled and fell into the evergreens. As he struggled to regain his footing he turned to see the leader of the punk-group reaching down for him. He braced himself for the expected attack.

"Don't worry old man, I'm not going to hurt you this time," he said. The young man spoke very softly offering his help. Carl got up. The young man reached into his pocket and slowly pulled out a crumpled bag and handed to Carl. "What is this?" asked Carl. "It is all of your stuff," the man explained, It's all of the stuff we took including your wallet and your money." "I don't understand," Carl said, "Why would you help me now?"

The man shifted his feet, seemly embarrassed and very comfortable, as he began to speak. "I learned something from you" he said. "I ran with that gang and hurt people like you. We picked on you because you were old and we knew we could get away with it. But every time we came and did something to you, instead of yelling and fighting back you offered us a drink of water.

You didn't hate us for tormenting you. You kept showing love in spite of what we did. The young man stopped for a moment, sighed and said, "I couldn't sleep after we stole your stuff so I'm bringing it back." He paused for another moment, not knowing what to say, and finally he said, "That bag is my way of saying thanks for straightening me out." Then he turned and walked away.

Carl looked at the bag in his hands and gingerly opened it. He took out his gold retirement watch and put it back on his wrist. He opened the wallet and checked his wedding picture. He gazed for a moment at the young bride who smiled back at him after all those years.

Carl died a couple of days before Christmas. Many of his friends came to calling hour and to the funeral. At the service the minister noticed a tall young man, who he didn't recognize, sitting quietly in the rear corner of the church. During the sermon the minister spoke of **Carl's Garden, A Lesson In Life.** In a voice made with thick unshed tears he said, "Do your best and make your garden as beautiful as you can. We will never forget Carl's garden."

The following spring another announcement was made in the Sunday bulletin, it read, **Person needed to care for Carl's Garden.** The announcement went unheeded by members of the church until one day there was knock on the Pastor's door. Opening the door the minister saw a man he thought he recognized. "I believe this is my job, if you will have me," the young man said.

The young man went to work and over the next several years he tended the flowers and shrubs just like Carl had done. During that time he finished high school, went on to college, and even got married. He joined in the community projects and became a leader in his hometown. He never forgot his promise to Carl's memory and kept the garden just like Carl would have done.

One day the young man came to see the minister and explained that he could no longer care for the gardens. He said with a shy and happy smile, "My wife just had a baby boy and we are bringing him home tomorrow." "Congratulations," said the minister as he accepted the keys to the garden shed. "That is wonderful! What is the baby's name?" "Carl, we named him Carl." he replied.

That is the whole Gospel Message, simply told.

AUTUMN BEGINS

The Fall Season

September is almost over and we can say the we have enjoyed a relatively good summer. The temperatures have been mild, we have enjoyed a fair amount of rainfall, enough to keep the lawns green without too much sprinkling and the gardens haven't been baked into weed patches. Unfortunately, this hasn't been true for other sections of the country. The corn and bean crops in the Midwest have suffered dreadfully from the droughts, while other parts of the country have received an unseasonal amount of rain.

A season is a subdivision of the year marked by the changes in the weather, ecology, and the hours of sunlight that we receive. Seasons are determined by both the astronomers and the meteorologists. Astronomers determine the exact times that the Sun crosses the tropics of Cancer and Capricorn and when it crosses the equator to determine the equinox, at which time we enjoy equal lengths of days and nights. The meteorologists observe and forecast the weather. They add additional seasons such as the Dry Season, the Wet Season, the Thunderstorm Season, the Tornado Season and even the Hurricane Season.

During the spring, March, April and May the northern hemisphere has a warming of temperatures because of the intensity of the sunlight that reaches the Earth's surface. Animals who have hibernated during the winter began to stir, birds start their migration, and plants begin to grow. Even the grass turns green, provided the weatherman delivers the proper amount of rain. Thus the meteorologist gets involved because he may announce we are having a rainy season, a hot season, or a dry season, which will certainly effect things.

On September 22, according to the astronomers, the Sun has reached the solstice that will cause a lessening of sunlight and a change from summer to autumn occurs. Many think that autumn is the best time of year. The lawns are all in, the gardens have produced their limits, even the pumpkins are beginning to turn orange preparing for Halloween. We who live in New England are blessed with the change in the leaves. The maple trees, the oak trees and other similar deciduous trees turn the land into a cornucopia of color. Many say that it takes a stroke of Jack Frost's wand to illuminate the hue. Others say that it is caused by the change of the sunlight. In any event we can all agree that it is God's handiwork as evidence. It is the season.

In Paul's letter to his apostle Timothy we find these words:

> "Preach the Word:
> Be prepared in season
> And out of season;
> Correct, rebuke and encourage,
> With great patience and careful instruction.
> For the time will come
> When men will not put up with
> Sound doctrine"

ELECTION DAY

Election Day is Tuesday November 5. The future of our country depends on your prayerful consideration of the candidates seeking elected office and of you exercising your privilege to vote. We urge you to vote. Furthermore, if possible offer to help others to the polling place.

> **Remember this Proverb: "When the righteous triumph there is great elation: but when the wicked rise to power, men go into hiding."**
>
> Proverb 28:12

THANKSGIVING

Harvest Festival
Third Thursday in November

Thanksgiving Day is a harvest festival. It is a time to give thanks for that which we have received through the bounty of God, our Father. It is a holiday that is celebrated primarily in the United States and Canada. While it has a **religious** origin, Thanksgiving is principally identified as a **secular holiday.** That is to do with the things of the world, not spiritual or under church control. The airlines look forward to Thanksgiving because it is the busiest travel time of the year.

It seems like the month of November is a bridge between two of the biggest commercial events of the year—**Halloween** and **Christmas**, with **Thanksgiving** stuck right in the middle. For many, Thanksgiving is a melody of **over eating;** turkey and dressing, cranberry sauce, mash-potatoes and gravy, including corn pudding, sweet potatoes, green beans, squash, followed by pumpkin pie or pecan pie with whipped cream. Hum, makes you hungry to think about it. Did you know that more than 300 million turkeys are raised in the United States each year with an estimated 40 million consumed on Thanksgiving Day?

In **1621**, after a hard and devastating first year in the New World, the Pilgrims' fall harvest was very successful and plentiful. There was corn, fruits, vegetables of all kinds, fish and meat that had been packed in salt or smoke cured over fires. They had enough food put away in stores to last through the coming winter. The pilgrims had beaten the odds. They built homes in the wilderness, they raised enough crops to keep themselves alive, and they were at peace with their neighbors. **Governor William Bradford,** proclaimed a day of thanksgiving that was to be shared by all of the people in the colony, including their neighboring native American Indians.

The celebration of an annual gathering held following the harvest time went on for years. During the **American Revolution,** circa 1770, a day of national thanksgiving was suggested by the Continental Congress.

In **1863,** President Abraham Lincoln proclaimed a national day of thanksgiving, and since that time each President has issued a Thanksgiving proclamation, usually designating the fourth Thursday of November as the special holiday.

Thanksgiving is a time to thank God for all of the good things that he has bestowed upon us—the love and care of family members and friends; a healthy life, a successful career, a loving wife, caring children, and so many more blessings that we have received.

Closing prayer

CHRISTMAS IS COMING

December 25

Christmas is coming! I am reminded of the old familiar poem by Norman Williams

> Christmas is Coming
> Christmas is coming. The goose is getting fat.
> Please put a penny in the old man's hat.
> If you haven't got a penny, a ha'penny will do.
> If you haven't got a ha'penny, God bless you."

It is important at this time of year that we reflect on the meaning of Christmas and the events leading up to that special day, **December 25th.** What is Christmas? What does Christmas mean to us? Many in our society would like us to change the name of **Christmas** to the word **Holiday.** Have we lost the passion for celebrating the birth of Jesus Christ and care more about being politically correct, so as not to offend anyone? Instead of hearing "Merry Christmas" we hear "Happy Holidays", or instead of lighting the Christmas Tree we "turn on" the Holiday tree.

The word CHRISTMAS is formed from two words, Christ+Mass, meaning a mass or religious service in commemoration of the birth of Jesus Christ. History tells us that December 25 was designated Christmas Day by Constantine in the year 325 AD. The actual date of Jesus' birth is unknown. Christmas is celebrated by most Protestant and Catholic churches on the 25th of December. Eastern Orthodox churches celebrate Christmas on January 6 and the Armenian churches have Christmas on January 19th.

Many Christian churches have a period of preparation for Christmas that is known as ADVENT. It is a time when Christians make ready for the celebration of the birth of Jesus and anticipate His return to earth. It is a time that is rich with tradition and symbolism. It is a period of lighting candles, counting the days, waiting with hopeful hearts for the coming of Christ.

Advent begins four weeks before Christmas. Each Lord's Day during Advent a circular wreath of evergreen, is used. With candles interspersed, the wreath represents the circle of the year and life that endures through the winter months. The candles are lighted to give thanks to God.

> The first candle is the **HOPE Candle.** It is usually purple in color and symbolizes our faith in God.
> The second candle is the **BETHLEHEM Candle,** depicting the Christ child's cradle. This candle is called the **LOVE candle** and is blue in color.
> The third candle is the **SHEPHERD'S Candle** and it is either pink or rose. This candle typifies the act of sharing Christ. The candle is also known as the **JOY Candle.**
> The fourth candle is the **ANGEL'S Candle.** It is the candle of love and the final coming. It is also known as the **PEACE Candle.** It is usually colored red.
> The largest candle, colored white, is placed in the center of the wreath and is called the **CHRIST Candle.** It is traditionally lit on Christmas Eve.

In lighting Christmas candles and Christmas lights we are reminded that Jesus Is the light of the world . . . the light that we should follow. Scripture reminds us of what Jesus said:

> *"I am the light for the world. Follow me and you won't be walking in the dark. You will have the light that gives life."*
> John 8:12

There are many more symbols of Christmas. The fir tree or evergreen tree. At this time of year the leaves of most trees have turned red, yellow or brown and have fallen from their branches. The evergreen tree keeps its fresh green look and we adorn it with ornaments and lights symbolizing **LIFE.**

The custom of the Christmas Tree was brought to the United States by the Pennsylvania Germans in the 1820's. In 1923 President Calvin Coolidge held the first lighting of the White House tree. It started a long standing tradition that has continued to this day. The White House tree is a giant spruce that stands nearly 50 feet tall and is decorated with more than 15,000 lights.

There are many more things that remind us of the birth of Christ. They include the Christmas Bells; Candles; Advent Calendar; Christmas greeting cards and letters; Nativity scenes; Mistletoe, Ivy, Yule logs; Christmas chocolates and yes even candy canes. And many more.

It is great to reflect on the memories of Christmas past. Joyful memories I trust. But for those of us who sincerely wish to observe the season properly we need to put Christ back into our lives and remember that it is He who brings light into the darkness. He is the truth and the light of the way. Let's put <u>Christ</u> back into Christ<u>mas</u>.

GOD BLESS YOU, MAY EACH AND EVERYONE HAVE
A VERY MERRY CHRISTMAS.

2 Chronicles 7: 14 "If my people who are called by my name, will humble themselves and pray and seek my face and turn from their wicked ways, then I will hear from heaven and will Forgive their sin and will heal their land."

Author: Ezra

What is In The Backpack?

Invite all of the children to come to the front of the church and be seated on the steps.

Introduction: Question the children by asking, "Do you have a back—pack that you carry to school?" For those who do not, reassure them that someday they will and it will probably be carried on the school bus or in their car.

2. Ask those who carry-back packs, "What do you carry in your back-pack?" Answers may include; books, homework, reading assignments, note book paper, pencils, and maybe even include their lunch, a midday snack, or even a peanut-butter and jelly sandwich.
3. Leader then pulls up his back pack and explains that he may have some other items they haven't included. He begins to pull things out the back-pack, a band-aid, a can of soda, a church financial report, an old sermon, a favorite poem, a small flashlight and finally a "Red Bible."
4. Tell the story of the Red Bible. An old preacher who was dearly loved by everyone in the church carried a Red Bible. One day someone asked him, "Pastor Miller, why do your carry a red Bible?"
   He answered with a smile and said, **"No matter what color your Bible is, it should always be READ."**
5. Do you sometimes carry a Bible in your back pack?

Challenge: Spend more time with people over age 70 and under age 6.

Close with Prayer

Why Do We Come To Church?

Introduction: Question the children about church worship.

1. Why do we come to Church?
   If one of the answers is that we come to Church to worship God, ask the questions: How do we worship God? In our singing, in our prayers by taking communion, by hearing the Gospel message, in reading the Bible, by fellowshipping with other Christians, and by bringing our tithes and offerings.
2. How do we talk with God? By prayer.
3. Does God talk with us? How?
   At this point have the cell phone in your pocket begins to ring. After a couple of rings, excuse yourself for the interruption and answer the the phone.
   "Hello!" Oh yes. Good morning. It certainly is nice of you to call. I am talking with the children of the church right now and we have been discussing how we worship. Is there a message that I can give them?"
   Good! I will pass that along to them. Thank you for your call."

Hang up the phone and turn to the children and say:

"That was God. He said that he knew that you were here in Church this morning and He said to tell you that HE LOVES YOU!"

Close with prayer.

ODE TO THE WINGS OF GOLD

A Naval Aviator's wings of gold,
When pinned on his chest with pride.
Will never come off, whether seen or not,
For they are there until he dies.

Those wings, though metal, are fused to the soul.
With adrenaline, adversity and froth.
No one can deny the feelings received,
When he successfully completes the loft.

In the world of flying, a life time of stories,
Of memories of ship-mates and friends.
Feelings last long after the flights are gone,
And the duty assignments have end.

When the flight suit is hung in the closet with care,
The Wings of Gold still exist.
A Naval Aviator's bearing speaks of what was,
But his heart clearly speaks of what is.

Go Navy!

Al Schmid
LCDR USNR

HIGH FLIGHT

Oh! I have slipped the surly bonds of Earth,
And danced the skies on laughter-silvered wings,
Sunward I've climbed, and joined the tumbling mirth.
Of sun split clouds—and done a hundred things,

You have not dreamed of—wheeled and soared and swung.
High in the sunlit silence. Hovering there.
I've chased the shouting wind along, and flung
Meager craft through footless halls of air.
Up, up the long delirious, burning blue,
I've topped the wind-swept heights with easy grace,
Where never lark or even eagles flew—

And while with silent, lifting mind I've trod,

The high untrespassed sanctity of space,
Put out my hand and touched the face of God.

John Magee

A BUMPY RIDE

"My help comes from the Lord, who made heaven and earth."
Psalm 121: 2 (NKJV)

In all of the years of my flying career there have been several experiences that are memorable and they have taught me important lessons. One such experience happened on a flight from Windsor Locks, Connecticut to Tucson, Arizona. I was not flying as a crew member but as a passenger aboard a commercial airline. My co-pilot and I were going to Tucson to the Gates Learjet factory to pick up a new Learjet 35 and ferry it back to Bradley Field, Connecticut.

The plan was to fly from Bradley Field to St. Louis, Lambert Airport, change flights and continue on to Tucson, Arizona. We had a brief layover in St. Louis and while we were waiting in the passenger lounge I noticed a young boy, also waiting to board the flight. He was about the age of my youngest son who was six years old. It became apparent that he was traveling alone.

When the flight was called, the young boy was escorted ahead of the other passengers to find his seat. When I got to the cabin I discovered that my seat assignment was next to his. We put our bags in the overhead baggage compartment and settled down to getting ready for the flight. I noticed that the boy seemed very confident and relaxed and spent some time coloring in an airline coloring book. We engaged in a conversation and he said that he was going to Tucson to visit his grand-mother. He showed neither anxiety nor worry about the flight, perhaps he had done this trip before.

The taxi out from the gate to the active runway was routine. The takeoff was smooth and the jetliner climbed quickly to its cruising altitude of 35,000 feet. Lunch was served and we enjoyed some small talk as we flew westward. After about an hour and a half the airplane flew into some dark clouds and into a nasty storm. The airplane bounced and twisted like a kite in the wind. The air turbulence was moderate and the pitching and the lurching of the aircraft began to frighten some of the passengers. I looked over at the boy and he didn't seem to be upset and was taking it all in stride.

A lady passenger across the aisle became alarmed by the bumpy ride and asked the little boy if he were scared. "No ma'am." he replied looking up briefly from his coloring book. "My dad is the pilot."

There are times when events in our lives make us feel like we are in the middle of a bad storm. Try as we may we cannot seem to understand or to cope with the turbulence that surrounds us. We wish to get our feet on solid ground. We have the sensation of being suspended in mid-air with nothing to hold on to, nothing to stand on and no certain way to get to safety.

In the middle of the storm, however, we can remember that our Heavenly Father is our pilot. Despite the circumstances our lives are in the hands of the One who created heaven and earth.

If uncontrollable fear or grief begins to rise within you today, simply say to yourself, "My Dad's the pilot." And your flight will be blessed.

MAY DAY, A SECULAR OR RELIGIOUS HOLIDAY

May Day, celebrated on the first of May, is a day that is observed in the northern hemi-sphere as a spring festival time. It is usually a public holiday. It is a celebration of the end of winter and a proclamation of the beginning of spring.

May Day is related to the Celtic festival of **Beltane** or the Germanic festival of **Walpurgis Night.** May Day falls exactly a half year from November to May and was significant in the pagan worship of northern European cultures. It has traditionally been an occasion for popular and often raucous celebrations.

As Europe became Christianized the pagan holidays lost their religious character and either changed into popular secular celebrations, like **May Day**, or were merged with or replaced by new Christian holidays such as *Christmas, Easter, Pentecost and All Saints Day.*

In the 20th Century many neo-pagans began reconstructing the old traditions and started to recognize **May Day** as a pagan-religious festival again. In moderation, the day became a more secular day and became known for its traditional dancing and for the famous **May Pole Dances,** including the crowning of a **Queen of May.**

In **Rome,** the Roman Catholics made the entire month of May a celebration and called it **Mary's Month** to honor the Blessed Virgin Mary. During this time special art displays were made and schools would have skits about Mary. The statutes of the Mother of Jesus would be adorned with flowers as a crown.

Other religious groups have a custom of having a May breakfast. At the May breakfast there are colorful May baskets made by the members containing flowering plants, candy and sweets, fudge and fancy flowers. Traditionally, a May basket would be left on a neighbor's doorstep. The givers rings the door bell and runs away. The person receiving the basket tries to catch the giver and if they are successful a Kiss was exchanged.

In **Ireland**, May Day has been celebrated since pagan times at the feast of Beltane. The name was later changed to **Mary's Day.** Bonfires were lit to mark the coming of summer and to banish the long nights of winter.

In **St. Andrews,** students would gather on the beach the evening before May first and at sunrise they would run into the North Sea. Often naked.

In **France**, on May 1, 1561 King Charles IX received a sprig of Lily-of-The Valley as a lucky charm. He decided to offer a lily of the valley each year to the ladies of the court. This tradition has continued through the centuries. It was customary for the lady receiving the sprig to give a kiss to the giver. And so it has been and will continue to be.

But **May Day** celebrations often are raucous. This year May 1 marked a day of protesting and violence throughout the country. One melee after another.

- In **Oakland,** the scene was violent with clashes between the activists and police. Police had to fire tear-gas and make arrests in order to maintain civil control.
- In **Seattle,** black clad protesters used base ball bats and clubs to break windows in stores in town, then ran amuck through the streets disrupting traffic.
- In **New York,** hundreds of demonstrators spilled out on to 5th Avenue declaring it a day that would mark a spring revival of their movement.
- In **Chicago,** more than 2,000 activists marched through the city demanding immigration reform.
- In **Atlanta,** about 100 people rallied outside the State Capital demanding change and promoting union activity.
- In **Providence,** a percussive, traffic stopping parade of more than 300 marchers joined to declare a "Day For The Workers." They wanted to remind the banks and corporations that "They would be nothing without their workers." May Day has been declared the **International Worker's Day.**

In our own day and age we are not likely to carve out graven images, or change long established traditions because we tend to serve our own self interests, seeking whatever it is we think we want . . . rather than the blessings God longs to give us. Even when we promise ourselves that we are going to obey the Lord, we have to be careful to add, **"If it be thy will Lord, I will . . . with God's help."**

> Holy Father, help us to put away everything that gets in the way of our relationship with you, especially our wrongful, selfish desires. Fill us so full of your Holy Spirit that there will be no more room for anything else. Amen.

WHAT WILL MATTER

Ready or not, someday it will all come to an end.

There will be no more sunrises, no minutes, no hours or days. All the things you have collected, whether treasured or forgotten, will pass to someone else.

Your wealth, fame and temporal power will shrivel to irrelevance. It will not matter what you owned or what you were owed. Your grudges, resentments, frustrations, and jealousies will finally disappear.

So too, your hopes and ambitions, plans, and to-do-lists will expire. The wins and losses that once seemed so important will fade away. It won't matter where you came from, or on what side of the tracks you lived. It won't matter whether you were beautiful or brilliant. Even your gender or skin color won't matter.

So what will matter? How will the value of your days be measured? What is relevant is not what you brought, but what you built. Not what you got, but what you gave. What will matter is not your success but your significance. Not what you learned but what you taught. What will matter is every act of integrity, compassion, courage or sacrifice that enriched, empowered or encouraged others to emulate your example.

What will matter is not your competence, but your character. What will matter is not how many people you knew, but how many people will feel a lasting loss when your are gone. What will matter is not your memories, but the memories that live in the hearts of those who loved you. What will matter is how long you will be remembered, by whom, and for what.

Living a life that matters doesn't happen by accident. It's not a matter of circumstance but of choice.

> *"Nothing in all creation is hidden from God's sight.*
> *Everything is uncovered and laid bare before the eyes of him*
> *to whom we must give account."*
>
> Hebrews 4:13

SKINNY DIPPING

During the Christmas Holidays, usually between Christmas and New Years, the Boy Scouts in central Illinois would return to Camp Illinek, the camp located on Lake Springfield, for a mid-winter rally and reunion. It was a great time to renew friendships, talk about how things were going at school, and recall the events of last summer's camping. We would talk about important things, like "What happened to your beautiful sun tan that you worked on all summer long? What are your plans when you finish college? and Who are you dating?" etc.

After lunch at the mess hall, when the dishes had been washed, the group would wend down to the water-front, to the boat house dock, to check on the boats and canoes that had been winterized and stored for next summer's activities. Remember the fun we had at general swim and how we took the canoes and row boats out on the lake after supper? All was well.

One year at the rally the weather had turned particularly mild. Unusual for Illinois in December. Most of the snow had melted and the lake was covered with a thin layer of smooth ice. A group of the waterfront staff met on the boat house dock and were reminiscing about the past summer when one of the group mentioned that it was time for "general swim". The sun was bright, the temperature in the mid-forties, and the lake was alluring. Even with a thin layer of ice it seemed like it would be okay for a quick dip.

Now you may have heard the cliché "One boy a whole boy, two boys a half-a-boy, and three boys, no boy at all." There were more than three boys standing on the boat house dock when it was announced "It's time for general swim." Not one to reject a challenge, the next voice that was heard said, **"I will if you will."** We all stripped down to our under shorts and stood on the edge of the dock. At the word **"go"** we all jumped in. Cur splash! Through the ice into the freezing water. General swim was never like this.

When we broke through the ice into the water my body felt like it had been hit with a red hot poker. We didn't know the meaning of thermal-hyperemia but we experienced it. It was the quickest swim I even made. I couldn't get back to the dock fast enough. We all clambered up on the boat house dock and with chattering teeth and shaking knees we all expressed what a wonderful experience it had been. No one would dare admit as to how impetus we had been or how foolish we were.

Proverbs provides us with these thoughts:

Vs 3 *"A man's own folly ruins his life, yet his heart rages against the Lord." Prov. 19: 3 Man* blames God for his troubles.

Vs 16 *"He who obeys instructions guards his life, but he who is contemptuous of his ways will die."*

Vs 20 *"Listen to advice and accept instructions, and in the end you will be wise."*

Vs 21 *"Many are the plans in a man's heart, but it is the Lord's purpose that prevails."*

THE NEED TO FLY

I watch as he turns to leave the hangar
His eyes scroll about as he takes it all in.
My heart feels the ties I know he is breaking,
I see a blink, then a tear as tries to grin.

Weather, flight plans, near and far lands,
That's how he has lived this gentleman
This decision, put off for so long
Says, "Let's wrap it up," that is the plan.

The love for all he is, hits me so hard,
Watching his face like a living cue card.
The list of his losses he alone must review,
Will he allow me to help him get through?

Thousands of miles across the great sky,
Loving the privilege of his own wings to fly,
Seeing the world from a lofty view,
While modestly saying, "Well that's what I do."

A surprise in the offing is what we both need.
Time for the grandkids, and each other indeed.
Homebodies on outings by car or by air.
It won't matter to me as long as he's there.

Leisurely outings not controlled by a clock.
A hand-hold stroll down some rustic dock.
Time to give back for all that has been,
Making room for each other away from life's din.

A prayer by Jabez was the very first glue.
Each was alone, but life is better by two.
This time in life may we spend it together.
This our own Autumn, life's sweetest weather.
Thank God for the blessings on this . . . our love

Audrey C. Schmid

LEAVE THE LIGHT ON MOMMY

When I was young and thought like a child,
Things scared me and my mind went wild.
Like when I was afraid, "What's under my bed."
Or things in the closet that I would dread

I often would jump two steps away
To land on my bed to be safe at bay.
But then I would look at the closet door,
And I knew inside there was so much more.

I would lie in bed with the light turned on,
Waiting for the comfort of my mom.
She would tuck me in and give me a kiss,
"Leave the light on mommy," I would insist.

She would smile at me and give me a hug,
And would try to leave, but I would give her a tug,
She would bend back down and whisper in my ear,
"Don't worry honey, there's nothing to fear."
Each year as I grew older I knew she was right,
But sometimes though they were just out of sight,
So I would talk to them and say, "BEWARE,"
Cause my Mother's around, and I don't scare.

William Benito 9/07

LINE OF LIFE

I was walking among the head-stones one day, when I had a little time.
Each one had the date of birth and death, separated by a line.
Some dates were quite far apart, Some just a month or two,
But each had a line, representing the time, of the life I never knew.

What kind of life did they live, in the line between the dates,
Were there other lives in that line, were there kids or other mates?
I read each one to find more clues of the line that meant their life,
Some said "Father, Mother, Son or Daughter, even Beloved Wife."

I wanted to know more about the line that came between the years.
Were there many happy times, or were there many tears?
Some had a Christian cross, to show that they'd been saved,
Others had a simple Cross or Star of David for the sacrifice they'd made.

Some said that 'They Would Be Missed,' or 'Until We Meet Again,'
But it never seemed to say by whom, or if they even had a friend.
Every stone had a line chiseled between the dates,
I wondered about each one I saw, as cars entered through the gates.

They spoke of all the things he'd done, the people he had touched,
I knew from all the tears that were shed, they loved him very much.
I watched as some forced smiles of the times that they recalled.
There were so many people there, hundreds all and all.

Their tears were shed and then they left, I found myself alone.
I walked over to the place of rest, and gazed upon the stone.
I wanted to know more about his life and of his many friends,
But there like others, just a line, with a date at either end.

William Benito 04

BE QUIET AND LISTEN

"The words of the wise heard in quietness . . . are better than the shouting of a ruler among fools."

Ecclesiastes 9: 17 (NASB)

Solomon, the writer of Ecclesiastes, was a wise and affective leader. He gained much wisdom and knowledge through his lifetime. God gave Solomon wisdom, but Solomon gained knowledge by observing and by developing his own attitudes toward life. It is well known, if only by common sense, that you cannot listen if you are talking. So, I dare say that Solomon was a good listener.

I am reminded of the cardinal rule that was observed at the dinner table in the ward room by the Navy pilots and officers as we ate our meals aboard ship or at the Naval Station. Three subjects that were forbidden and were never discussed were: Religion, Politics, and Sex. Someone once asked, "Well what else is there to talk about?" Perhaps we need to better understand the wisdom and attitudes of Solomon.

The passage in Ecclesiastes 9:17 bears witness to the fact that it is important to listen. It occurs to me that we have been engaged in an election year that seemingly has come to an end. The election is over but now we are asking the questions what is next. We have listened to the "shouting of candidates" and the various promises and declarations made by each until it is now time to "listen in quietness." As we regroup to begin the most important period in our history when it is critical to make the right decisions to sustain our country, its fate and our future, our freedoms and our well-being all which has been received from our God. We need to carefully and prayerfully consider our choices and act accordingly.

In order for the wise person to be heard there must first be silence of the listeners. This is in sharp contrast to those who have shouted in order to be heard above the drone of the foolish. Those who would rather argue than listen to the wisdom of the Lord are in great number. Be cautious about this. God gave us the ability to speak, the ability to reason and the ability to make good decisions. We also have another important gift and that is the ability to listen. We can learn how to live a righteous life and how to truly help one another if we chose to listen. This perhaps is our most precious gift. While it is true that we must speak to ask questions, there is a point that we must close our mouths and open our ears in order to comprehend the answers. We have exercised our right to vote and to be heard. We have chosen our new leaders, we must now remain committed to doing the job to our benefit and the Lord's satisfaction.

1. We must support pro-life legislation, because God hates the shedding of innocent blood. (Prov. 6:17)
2. We must continue to support our allies in Israel because God blesses those who bless Israel and curses those who don't. (Gen. 12: 3)
3. We must ask our government to work on debt reduction, because the Bible tells us that "The borrower is the servant to the lender." Prov. 22:
4. We must lower our unemployment rate because God says, "If a man does not work, let him not eat." (2 Thess. 3: 10)
5. We all must agree that our government's purpose is to reward the good and punish the evil. (Romans 13)
6. We must insist that our elected officials adhere as closely as possible to complying with God's word. (2 Timothy 3: 16)
7. And we should know that whoever was elected, God was the one who put them in that authority. (Dan 12:21)

I urge you to speak quietly but succinctly. At the same time think of the challenges we have as citizens of the United States of American and as children of God.

Amen.

CHOOSING IS EASIER WHEN YOU
UNDERSTAND THE RESULTS

**"For God so loved the world that he gave his one and only
son that whoever believes in him shall not perish but have
everlasting life."**

John 3: 16

The church was nearly filled to capacity Sunday evening. After having
sung several hymns the minister went to the pulpit and before he started
his sermon he paused to introduce a guest minister, who was attending
the service.

The Pastor told the congregation the guest minister was one of his
dearest childhood friends and that he wanted him to have a few moments
to greet the church members and to share whatever he felt would be
appropriate for the service.

Following the introduction an elderly man stepped up to the pulpit
and began to speak. He said:

"A father and his son and a friend of his son went sailing off the New
England coast one evening. As they sailed, a fast moving storm approached
the craft, the wind began to blow harder and harder, the sea became very
rough, the waves were so high that they could not return to the harbor.
Even though the father was an experienced sailor he could not keep the
boat upright and the three people on board were swept into the ocean as
the boat capsized."

The old man hesitated . . . made eye contact with two teenagers who
were for the first time in the service beginning to seem somewhat interested
in the story. The speaker continued: "Grabbing a rescue line, the father had
to make the most excruciating decision of his life. To which boy should he
first throw the line? He had only seconds to make a decision. The father
knew that his son was a Christian and he knew the other boy was not. The
agony of his decision could not be matched by the torrent of the rain and
raging waves. He had to throw the line, he had to make a choice.

"The father yelled out, 'I love you son!' Then he threw the rope to his son's friend. By the time he had pulled the friend back to the capsized boat, his son had disappeared beneath the water. His body was never recovered."

At this point the two teenagers in the pew were sitting straight up anxiously waiting for the next words to come out of the mouth of the old minister.

"The father," the preacher continued, "Knew his son would step into eternity with Jesus, but he could not bear the thought of his son's friend having to spend forever in damnation. He had sacrificed his own son in order to save the son's friend."

How great is the love of God that he should do the same for us? Our Heavenly Father sacrificed his one and only son that we could be saved. I urge you to accept His offer to rescue you by taking hold of the life-line that He is throwing to you.

Finished with his story the old minister turned and sat down in his chair. Silence filled the room. Then the young minister went to the pulpit and delivered a brief sermon, followed by a benediction.

Within minutes the two teenagers, who were so attentive, were at the old man's side. "Nice story," said the first teen, "But I don't think it was very realistic for a father to give up his only son's life in hope that the other boy would become a Christian."

"Well, you've got a point there," answered the old man as he glanced at his old worn Bible. "But I am standing here today to tell you this story to illustrate what it must have been for God to give up his son for me."

"You see . . . I was the father and your minister was my son's friend."

I would rather live my life as if there is a God and die to find out there isn't, than live live my life as if there isn't a God and die to find out there is.

The End